THE Keys TO JOY-FILLED LIVING

ROBERT C. JAMESON, MFT

New York

D0829785

THE *Keys* TO *Joy*-FILLED *Living*

BY ROBERT C. JAMESON, MFT

ISBN: 978-1-60037-467-8

Library of Congress Control Number: 2008929705

Published by:

MORGAN · JAMES
THE ENTREPRENEURIAL PUBLISHER ™
www.morganjamespublishing.com

Morgan James Publishing, LLC

1225 Franklin Ave. Ste 325

Garden City, NY 11530-1693

Toll Free 800-485-4943

www.MorganJamesPublishing.com

In an effort to support local communities, raise awareness and funds, Morgan James Publishing donates one percent of all book sales for the life of each book to Habitat for Humanity.

Get involved today, visit www.HelpHabitatForHumanity.org.

Cover & Interior Design by:
Bonnie Bushman
bbushman@bresnan.net

Dedication

To my wife Linda—my first editor, best supporter, and constant companion.

To my daughter Nicol and my wondrous grandson Dylan.

Acknowledgments

I would like to acknowledge my dear friend and mentor John-Roger for all the words of wisdom he has shared with me through time. He taught me so much about how to create joy in my life and how to have healthy relationships. He has been an inspiration for me to be my best, to have a voice, and to speak my truth with clarity and courage. Much of what I am presenting here is a reflection of his guidance. I must also acknowledge all of the clients I have had the honor of working with through the years. It has been a pleasure to learn from you. I am very grateful for the keen editing eyes of my dear friends Ed Mancini, Stephen Viens, and Russ Anderson. The three of you helped make this book presentable and readable. I must also acknowledge every author of every self-help book that I have read and those who walked before me. The staff at Morgan-James Publishing has been very inspirational in this project. Without your team, this book would not be in its current form. Thank you for saying yes. All along the way, many have encouraged me to put all my handouts into a book. I want to thank all of you for your confidence and your words of encouragement. I must also thank my brothers, Diamond and Gerry, and my mom and dad for loving me as I went through my own transformational process.

Contents

CONTENTS

CONTENTS

Preamble

*H*i! I'm human. If you are reading this, so are you. As humans, we have thoughts that bounce around in our heads. We can control some of these thoughts, but most we can't. These thoughts create feelings. We like some of our feelings, but there are some we want to control or get rid of. We also move through time. Time seems to regulate us. We often feel that there is either too much time or not enough time. Some of us are always late, but some of us are always early. Sometimes we live in the past, sometimes we live in the future, and sometimes we live in the present.

We also move through space. When we do, we bump into things—other creatures and other humans. We like some of the humans we bump into, and we do not like others. We spend time with the ones we like. We call these encounters relationships. Some relationships last a long time; some last only a short time. Some relationships end positively; many end with emotional pain or a sense of loss. All relationships are classrooms, and we get to learn in each one of them.

Certain other things about humans are important to know. We all have bodies. Sometimes we like our bodies, and sometimes we don't. One thing is for sure: we will have our bodies for our entire lives. We like and dislike other human bodies as well. We want to look at and touch the ones we like. Interaction is important to us. Some bodies we don't like. We don't want to get close to them. I guess we are afraid they will rub off on us and we will get their cooties. Fear is a big deal with us. It's one of our primary motivational points. We are afraid of being rejected by other humans because we really want to be accepted, loved, approved, and appreciated by other humans.

While we are here on this planet, we are in an informal school full-time. During each moment in this school, we have an opportunity to learn lessons. We may think some of the lessons are stupid and irrelevant to us. We think the ones we dislike are intended for other humans. We learn either by receiving information (the easiest way) or by having an experience (the more challenging way). Although it is the more difficult way to learn, we seem to prefer learning by having an experience. Usually, our growth is a process of trial and error, or experimentation. All of our experiences are important for our growth. Sometimes we don't want to grow anymore, so we get stuck in our ways, or our positions of rightness. We always do what we think is the right thing to do. Our behavior may seem illogical to others, but it is always perfectly logical to us. Some humans think they know everything even when they don't. Many times these people don't like listening to other people.

Our lessons are presented to us in various forms until we have learned what we need to learn. When we have learned what we need to learn, we get to move on to the next lesson. The learning never stops. As long as we are here, we have lessons to learn.

We often think what we don't have is better than what we do have. We sometimes think that our lives would be better if only we were over there, or if we had that, or if we were with some other person. What's funny is that when we get all those things we want, there is always another something else that we want. This is another one of those ongoing processes that never seems to end. Our eyes, ears, noses, mouths, and hands always want something new and different.

This entire planet is a mirror of how we see or feel about ourselves. We can't love or hate something unless it reflects something that we love or hate about ourselves. What we do with our lives is up to us.

We have the keys to create change. What we do with these keys and how we use them is a choice. We don't always know we have a choice, but we do. We often think we are stuck even when we're not. Each of us thinks we are the center of the universe. We wonder how each situation is going to help us. We prefer to talk about things that are important to us personally. If we think someone likes us, then we like them. We trust and believe them. Some humans never forget anything and hold onto everything. Some of us just don't remember anything. Some humans want to heal and create a better life; others just want to become numb and pretend they are someone else or are somewhere else. Some humans want to control everything because they think that will make them safe. Some feel they have to lie about everything to feel safe, important, or loved. We often wear social masks we created as children. If these masks were effective in early childhood, many of us, as adults, think they will continue to work in every situation we encounter. This is an area of big learning for most of us.

Behind our social masks, we are basically very much the same. All the answers to the questions we ask are inside us. We need to listen and trust our inner voice. We need to remember who and what we are. Even though we know all this, we tend to forget it easily. So keep moving through time and space. As you read through this book, I'm confident you will wake up and remember the keys to joy-filled living.

CHAPTER 1

Feelings

ow are you feeling?

Do you feel happy? Sad? Confused? Angry? Neutral?

How are you feeling? This question has so many answers. Most people respond, "Fine." Most people don't really want to hear how the person he or she asked is truly feeling, and the question is often just a way to say hi. When we are with people we really care about, however, we really do want to know how they are feeling. Their answers tell us how we are to respond to their words and actions. So a response of "fine" is inadequate for us. Unfortunately, most of us are in the habit of just saying "fine." After years of doing this, we lose contact with ourselves and our inner states of being. We don't know how we truly feel, and we no longer have the right words to accurately express what is going on inside.

There are many basic feelings—we can feel joyful, happy, sad, sorry, guilty, shameful, angry, hateful, fed up, fearful, scared, awful, disappointed, anxious, excited, needy, depressed, thankful, forgiving, neutral, peaceful, and the list goes on and on.

Feelings are colorful. By expressing our feelings, we communicate to the world what we like and dislike. Feelings are neither good nor bad; they just are. Feelings are emotions. Emotions equal energy in motion. Emotions are like the waves in the ocean. If you go with them, they can be pleasant, but if you resist or fight them, they can be scary.

So, how are you feeling? Look at the list of words below, and see if you can identify how you are feeling right now. Sometimes we feel more than one emotion at a time, and sometimes those emotions are opposites. If you are experiencing several different feelings right now, it doesn't mean you are weird or broken. It means you are human. Humans are complicated beings who often feel many different emotions at the same time. That's what makes being alive exciting and challenging. Also, feelings can change from moment to moment. In this exercise, I want you to identify what your dominant feelings are right now. If what you are feeling is not on the list, then just add your feeling to it. Don't limit your expression to what is printed below.

You might be asking, "Why do I want to know how I am feeling? How does it serve me? What is the purpose of putting a label on what I am feeling? It won't change my feelings. I'm just feeling. Isn't that enough? In fact, a lot of times I don't like what I am feeling. Sometimes, I don't want to feel."

By identifying or labeling what you are feeling, you create a point of awareness and an opportunity to take charge of that feeling. You can embellish it, you can diminish it, or you can observe it from a neutral point of view. Then you can take conscious control of your life. You will find out that you are not a victim of your feelings. You will learn to use them for your growth. So take a moment and circle or write in how you are feeling.

Aggressive	Agonized	Anxious	Angry
Arrogant	Bashful	Blissful	Bored
Cautious	Cold	Confident	Confused

Curious	Demure	Depressed	Disappointed
Disapproving	Disbelieving	Disgusted	Distasteful
Eavesdropping	Ecstatic	Enraged	Envious
Exasperated	Exhausted	Frightened	Frustrated
Grieving	Guilty	Happy	Horrified
Hot	Hung Over	Hurt	Hysterical
Idiotic	Indifferent	Innocent	Interested
Jealous	Loaded	Lonely	Love Struck
Meditative	Mischievous	Miserable	Negative
Obstinate	Optimistic	Overwhelmed	Paranoid
Perplexed	Pissed	Puzzled	Regretful
Relieved	Sad	Shameful	Shy
Shocked	Smug	Surly	Surprised
Suspicious	Sympathetic	Withdrawn	Worried

After you identify your dominant feelings, you can determine the intensity of what you are feeling on a scale of 1 to 10. This will give you information or awareness on what is going on inside of you in a measurable way and will give you a start on dealing with your feelings.

1   2   3   4   5   6   7   8   9   10

No Feeling   Moderate Feeling   Intense Feeling

AWARENESS

Awareness is the first step to change. We can't change anything until we are aware of it. If you look at a picture of an iceberg, you see only a small portion of it above the water; most of it is under the water. This is a classic symbol for the human consciousness. What is below the surface symbolizes our unconsciousness. We can't do anything with this part of us. Yet, it is what runs us. When our unconscious becomes conscious, we can begin to address it in one way or another. The point of awareness is what is right at the water's edge. The exercise above of identifying a word for what we are feeling and the intensity of that feeling is a process of bringing your unconscious to a point of awareness.

You say, "OK. That's great. Now I know that I'm mad as hell and I'm a 7.3! Now what? I don't feel any better. In fact, now I realize that I'm not a 7.3 but a 9.6, and if I keep talking I just might break a 10, so your exercise is not helping me at all. I'm aware, all right. I'm aware I don't like feeling this, and I'm still mad."

My response is, "I hear you." The questions I am hearing you ask are, "What do I do with this emotion?" and "How do I get out of this negative emotional state and into a positive place?"

So, let's take another step forward. I'm going to suggest something that might sound radical to you at first, and I would ask you to be a scientist and just check out what I'm going to suggest. Don't just think about it. Go out there in the world and look. Really check it out. Be very rigorous in your research.

I am going to suggest that you take a closer look at how you use your emotional state as a tool to get people, places, animals, and things to do what you want. You are included in the "people" category, by the way. I am going to limit my explanation to just people, in order to simplify my discussion, but everything I suggest also applies to places, animals, and things.

If people do or say what you want, you will have a positive emotional response. This part of the equation is just fine. Most of us are happy to have a positive emotional response. It's the other side of the equation that disturbs us. If people don't do or say what we want, we have a negative emotional response. We get angry, hoping we can create change through intimidation, or we have hurt feelings, hoping we can achieve change by creating guilt. That's it. This might seem simplistic, and I must admit that it is. And I want you to check it out. Watch what people do when they don't get what they want. What do you do when you don't get what you want? I am suggesting that humans have two primary responses when they don't get what they want. The "negatively charged" words listed above are subcategories of these two primary responses.

I am not suggesting that getting angry or having hurt feelings are the most effective approaches that we can use. They just seem to be two of the most basic tools we humans use to get what we want. Other tools are more effective at getting what we want, and I will present some of these tools later in the book.

Right now we are still in the process of becoming aware. We are in the process of discovering what we do and what we don't do. As I said before, the first step to change will always be awareness. As we continue to explore this idea, of using our emotions as tools to get what we want, I'm going to initially look at anger because it is the easier of the two to understand, and then I will discuss how we use hurt feelings.

ANGER

Anger, as I stated earlier, is a tool we use to get what we want. If I ask you to sit down and relax, and you do as I ask, then I have no reason to be angry with you. We could stay in a place of loving. If, however, you say, "No," then I have to ask you again, increasing the intensity of my voice until I am shouting. If you still refuse to do what I want you to do, then I will have to physically pick you up and set you where I want you to be.

The good news about anger is that it works. We can, and do, get people to do what we want them to do with our anger. There is also bad news with anger, and that is that it works. I have now created a habit. In order for me to get you to do what I want you to do, I have to get angry with you. Then, I do what is called transfer learning. In order for me to get all the people I see in the world to do what I want them to do, I have to get angry with them. Then I'm angry all the time, and that is a difficult way to go through life.

I am suggesting we have a belief that says we can get what we want if we get angry. Check this out. The next time you are angry, or irritated, or upset, or whatever word you want to describe it, ask yourself, "What do I want? Is being angry going to get me what I want?"

You might be driving down the freeway and some guy pulls in front of you, and all of a sudden you find yourself yelling and cursing at him. What do you want? Besides wanting to smash his car, you might just want him to give you some room and to be safe so you can get home in one piece. Will yelling and screaming get you what you want? I doubt it.

Or maybe some people you care about said or did something that you did not want them to do, and now you are yelling and cursing at them. What do you want? Will getting angry at them get you what you want? You could say, "Yeah, it will teach them a lesson so they will be nice to me in the future." Are you nice to people who yell and scream at you? What makes you think it will work with others? Maybe you just want them to be nice to you, to love you, and to respect you as a human being. Will anger get you these things? Again, I doubt it.

"OK," you say, "I get your point, but what do I do with all of my anger?" Good question. Let's look at a few situations as a way of answering this question.

Let's imagine you say or do something that I do not want you to say or do. That information comes over to me and I catch it. When I catch it, I choose to use the information however I choose to use it The decision is made extremely quickly. However, there is a choice point in there. Most people are not aware of this choice point, and they just react as if on automatic pilot. They have a habit that was formed years ago.

I catch the information that you are sending me, and it is not what I want to hear or see. I want you to say or do something different. Therefore, I react, and now I am angry. I take *my* anger and throw it at you, and you react with anger as well because now I am not saying or doing what you want me to say or do. You take *your* anger and throw it back at me, and now we are in a fight. Who wins? Whoever is either physically or verbally the strongest wins. This actually turns out to be a "lose-lose" situation.

This is the way most of us react to our world on a personal level and on an international or suprapersonal level. It's called war, and in my estimation, it does not work.

Let's look at another situation and see if we can take another step toward understanding anger.

Again, let's imagine you say or do something that I do not want you to say or do. This time, however, when I catch it, I realize I can choose to use this information any way I want. I choose to react with anger. It's a habit. I know, however, it has nothing to do with you. I know it's all my stuff, so rather than throwing it at you, I decide to suppress my anger.

However, if I suppress my anger, it will come out another way. It might come out as a cold, arthritis, ulcers, temporomandibular joint dysfunction, cancer, drug abuse, alcohol abuse, sugar abuse, food abuse, an accident, depression, revenge, or some other way. You can be sure that it will come out sooner or later, one way or another.

The question is, How can we express our anger in a way that we do not hurt others or ourselves? As I said earlier, anger is just a human emotion. It is not necessarily bad or good. It is just an emotion that is telling us that we are not getting what we want.

Let's look at yet another situation to further understand the process of anger. Once again, imagine you say or do something I do not want you to say or do. I catch it, and I react with anger. It is still a habit with me. I realize it has nothing to do with you. It's all mine. I take a moment and express my anger in a way that does not hurt me or you, and in the process I become very clear on what it is that I want from you. I go back to you and tell you what I want. You respond with some swear words, and I am angry again. I take another moment and express my anger away from you, again getting clear on what I want from you. I might say, "I just want you to be nice to me, and I don't want you to swear at me." Again, you respond with more swear words. Once more, I react with anger, express my anger away from you, and tell you what I want. If I am healthy, at some point in time, I will realize that I can't get what I want from you, and I will probably say to you, "Goodbye. God bless you, I love you, and goodbye."

Before I explore how we can express our anger without hurting others or ourselves, I want to discuss the dynamics of hurt feelings.

HURT FEELINGS

Feeling hurt is a basic human emotion that we all have experienced. It's not good or bad; it just is an emotion. As I suggested earlier, it's one of the things we do when we don't get what we want. I know I am walking on thin ice because some people hold their hurt feelings very close to their hearts. They feel justified in having them, and that's just fine with me. I am going to explore and explain how we use our hurt feelings to get others to do what we want. However, I am going to explain the flow of events so you can see and understand the process of hurt feelings.

Let's say you say to me, "I hate you and I don't ever want to see you again." Those are some of the hardest words anyone could ever hear. When those words come to me, I have a choice of how I am going to use that information. Again, this choice happens very quickly, and I acknowledge most of us are not aware that it exists. If you watch, however, you can see the decision process. So, I have a choice. How am I going to use this information? I could say to myself, "Thank you for sharing that with me. I appreciate your honesty. Goodbye. Have a wonderful life." I am aware most of us don't do that. However, it is a choice. We could respond in this manner. Or I could take that same information, "You don't love me anymore and you are going to leave me," and I could hurt my feelings with it. You don't hurt me, I do. You don't have the power to hurt my feelings. I hurt my feelings. As I am hurting my feelings, I am looking at you through my tear-filled eyes, and I notice that you are feeling guilty. If I am doing a really good job of hurting my feelings, you will feel really guilty, and you'll say, "Oh Robert, I'm sorry. I didn't really mean it. I'll take you back." At that time, I will begin to smile, and deep inside myself I say, "Gotcha. Now all I have to do to get you to do what I want is to hurt my feelings." Hurt feelings are sideways anger we use to get people, including ourselves, to do what we want through guilt.

I am not suggesting that this is a conscious process. It's something we learned to do when we were little babies. It just sits inside waiting to be used when necessary in order for us to get what we want. What we want from someone else can be an honest or a basic request, such as "I just want you to be nice to me." It doesn't have to be a bad or selfish thing.

As with anger, once we are in our hurt, we need to express our hurt in an effective way that does not hurt others or ourselves.

EXPRESSING ANGER AND HURT FEELINGS

Anger and hurt feelings seem to be stored in four places: the physical body, the emotions, the mind, and the unconscious. The exercise that I am about to share with you will clear all of the areas except the physical body. This exercise will lessen the tension in the body and therefore affect how your body feels. However, it will not give you the physical release that you might receive from taking a brisk walk or a yoga class.

I want you to do some writing. I want you to write from the point of view of you being a victim and to blame others for your troubles, your pain, your anger, and your hurt feelings. I am not suggesting you run your life from this point of view. I would encourage you to be responsible and accountable for your life, but in this exercise I want you to write from the victim's point of view.

There is a part of us that I call the *basic self* or the *child within*, and that part feels it has been victimized. I am asking you to allow that part of you to speak its truth.

I also want you to use a lot of four-letter words. When we start using swear words that we are not supposed to use, but that we all use, it begins to allow us to express some of that rage or deep hurt that is just sitting there below the surface. As you are doing your writing, there might be a time when you are just scribbling words on the paper and you can't even read what you are writing. That is just great because I <u>do not</u> want you to read what you write.

The process of writing gets all the negative stuff out. The process of reading puts it all right back in. Many people are not aware of this, so they write in their journals and keep them on their shelves to be read later. They will think about and analyze their issues as they reread their writing. When they do this, they just keep going over and over the same issues. They never seem to be able to get rid of the issue because they dump it and then reclaim it.

Again, do *not* read what you write. Some people are very creative and say, "But sometimes I write really neat stuff and I want to keep it for a poem, or a song, or something." That is fine. If you are this type of person, then all you have to do is keep another sheet of paper next to you as you do your anger writing, and if something comes up that you want to keep, just write it on this separate sheet of paper.

Once again, do *not* read what you write. I want you to do one of two things with your writing: tear it up and throw it away, or burn it. Some safe places to burn are the kitchen sink, the toilet, an ashtray, or the fireplace. Be careful and don't burn yourself or your house. Some smoke alarms are very sensitive, so just be aware. I encourage you to be a scientist and try both the tearing and the burning. See which one you like best. Some people like to tear, and some people like to burn. Some people like to tear and burn. Find out what works best for you.

There are two reasons I want you to tear or burn your writing. The first reason is that if you think someone just might read what you are writing, you will start censoring what you write. Another concept comes into play here: we are not held responsible for what passes through our minds. We are, however, held responsible for what we hold onto. So you could be writing some pretty foul stuff, and if you are afraid someone might read what you are writing, including yourself, you will hold onto those thoughts. If, however, you are certain that no one will read your writing, then you will begin to feel free to write whatever comes to your mind, no matter how ugly the thought. You will know that those ugly thoughts are just thoughts. We all think ugly thoughts from time to time, and we can just say "next." More stuff. "Next." When you do this exercise, know you are in the process of releasing things that you have been holding onto for a long, long time.

The second reason I want you to tear or burn your writings is a little subtler. You will have to watch for this one. After you have written out your anger and you have torn or burnt the writings, there will be a little feeling inside that will say, "That's gone." That doesn't mean you will not have to write about the same subject more than once. Some subjects run so deep that you might have to write about them one hundred times. Each time you write about them, however, they will become more and more complete. You will have peeled off another layer on the proverbial onion.

Another part to this writing exercise is very important. As we start letting go of our negativity, it will feel like there is a hole inside. For some people, this hole feels like a void and a great sadness can be felt. It is like, "Wow, a lot has happened to me." And with this void, tears can come. If that happens, that is great. Now the body is coming into the process, and it is beginning to heal itself, as well as your emotions, mind, and unconscious.

Beyond feeling the void, I want you to plant a seed. The seed is going to be in the form of an affirmation. In the big picture, what you are doing is getting rid of what you don't want and putting in what you do want. The affirmation that I want you to work with is very specific. I also want you to place your hands on your abdomen, just over your belly button, as you say the affirmation. When we place our hands on our abdomen, there is a feeling of protection and nurturing, and our little basic self or child within feels safe and nurtured and says, "Yeah, what do you want?"

Now that we have your basic self or inner child's attention, the affirmation is this: "(Your name), I am loving you. I am loving you, (Your name)." The wording is important to note. You are not saying, "I love you," because you just might not be in a loving place with yourself, in which case that part that knows and would say, "You don't love me. You hate me!" However, if you say, "I am loving you," the very statement is a loving act and cannot be denied. That little basic self or inner child will say, "Thank you. I need that."

For some people, the idea of talking to oneself is a very uncomfortable thing. Again, I would ask you to be a scientist and just check it out. Place your hands on your abdomen and say to yourself (either out loud or to yourself, whichever feels more comfortable): "(Your name), I am loving you. I am loving you, (Your name)." Say this affirmation about 20 to 25 times or until you feel full inside. And then every night before you go to sleep, place your hands on your abdomen and again say this affirmation until you feel full.

I would encourage you to write, tear and burn, and say your affirmations at least once every day for two weeks. When you do this process for this length of time, you will be able to release old issues that you may have been holding onto for years.

If you find that you are not angry or feeling hurt, just let yourself write about whatever comes up in a free-form writing style. Look at issues with your parents, past lovers, past or present bosses. Whatever comes up is just fine. This can become a very enjoyable process and a very healthy and effective way of dealing with your anger and hurt feelings.

DIRTY JARS AND BAKING CAKES

For some people, the process of writing, burning or tearing, and placing their hands on their abdomens while saying a nurturing affirmation brings up a lot of old feelings and memories that have been hidden down in the unconscious. The very thought of remembering and refeeling old history can be overwhelming and terrifying. We use a tremendous amount of energy holding these thoughts down in hopes they will just go away and leave us alone. I certainly understand the natural reflex to avoid unpleasant memories; unfortunately, this method of denial is not effective in creating health or joy in our lives. Strange as it sounds, it is helpful and healing to relook at and release these memories through this process. It's like you are cleaning your house and taking out the garbage. You are breaking through your denial system and seeing and feeling what is present in your life. I would like to share two little stories that might help you understand what is going on.

Let's say I have a jar in my hands. It is very dirty, inside and out, and I want it to be clean so I can reuse it to hold and carry something very precious. In order to clean this jar, I put some soap in it. I then get a brush and add a little water to help scrub away the dirt. After I scrub the jar inside and out, I put it under the faucet and turn on the water. I put clean water inside the jar, but that is not what comes out of the jar. What comes out of the jar is soap suds and dirty water. Now, I could say, "Oh, no! Soap suds and dirty water—turn the faucet off! I hate soap suds and dirty water. This is not working. I am turning this water off." If I do that, my jar will still be dirty, and I certainly won't want to put anything precious in it. It is a little cleaner, but now I am stuck with soap suds and dirty water, and no matter how long I wait, I will still have soap suds and dirty water. If I want the jar to be clean, I will have to turn the faucet on again and run clear water into the jar until it declares itself clean. "How long will that take?" you ask. As long as it takes. It will declare itself clean by the absence of soap suds and dirty water. If you look inside the jar, all the soap suds and dirty water are gone. All that is coming out of the jar is clean, clear water. If the jar is very dirty, it might require more soap and more scrubbing as well, which means you will have more soap suds and more dirty water. Each jar is different. The process of writing, burning or tearing, and holding on is very similar to cleaning out a dirty jar. We will know we are clean or clear inside when the anger or hurt is gone. A sense of peace just seems to show up inside. The residual memory might be there, but the emotional charge is gone.

Baking a cake is another way to look at the process of getting free from old emotional baggage. In order to bake a cake, we must first gather all the ingredients and all the utensils that are needed. Once we have everything on a counter, we could ask, "Do we have a cake?" No, not yet. We have our cookbook that tells us exactly how to make a cake, but we do not have a cake yet. We have to do something with all the stuff on the counter. We have to take action in the world. So, we preheat the over, mix all the dry ingredients and all the wet ingredients together, and pour them into a pan. We have already put a lot of work and time into this process. Again we could ask, "Do we have a cake?" No, not yet. We smell something, and we can taste something, but it is not cake yet. Do we stop here and get discouraged? If we do, we will not get cake. We will have an incomplete project. So, with as much determination as we can muster, we put our pan with the mixed ingredients into the oven to cook. Time passes. How much time? It depends on the type of cake we are cooking and the type of oven we are cooking in. If we pull our pan out before everything is cooked, we still will not have a cake. We will have something else. How will we know if our cake has cooked long enough? As my grandmother told me, "The cake tells you." She used a toothpick and her experience to determine if the cake was done. When we have taken the cake out of the oven, do we now have cake? My grandmother would say no. She never let me eat her cakes at this point. She told me I had to wait for it to cool down before I could eat it. Time passes. "I want my cake now!" I would say. "Have faith," she would tell me. "We need to put some frosting on it first, and it has to cool down in order for us to do that. After we put the frosting on the cake, then you can eat your cake." It was only after the frosting was on the cake that she called the process complete.

Many times we want to declare the process complete before it is, or we feel we have done enough and "should" have what we want now. If this begins to happen to you, just ask yourself, "Where in the process of making cake am I?" If you find yourself getting discouraged because of all the stuff that just seems to keep surfacing, you might want to remember the soap suds and dirty water story and say, "Oh boy, more soap suds!"

SOME AREAS TO WRITE ABOUT

- Agitation of the past
- Anything that bothers you
- Disharmony with a person or situation
- Someone or a situation at home, in your office, or in the world that annoys you
- Unwanted sounds in your head
- Anything that frightens you
- Judgments against yourself or others
- Unfulfilled expectations toward yourself or others
- Anything you have stuffed or repressed
- Anything you don't like
- Confusion about someone or something
- Any pain or discomfort in your body
- Anything that occurred that you wish had not occurred
- Feeling tired or exhausted
- Feeling hungry or a food craving
- Headache or a stomachache

- Any goal or dream you have not achieved

- Any procrastination

- Any disappointments or regrets

- Any misunderstandings

- Any unwanted emotions, thoughts, or physical disturbances

- Feelings of apathy, grief, fear, lust, or pride

- Resistance to goal setting

- Resistance to the goals themselves

- Resistance to action steps to completing goals

- Anything you are against

- Anything you are for

CATCH UP AND MAINTENANCE

There are two primary phases to expressing anger or hurt feelings. One I call the catch-up phase, and the other is called the maintenance phase.

The catch-up phase is when we first start the process of healing our current and past wounds. It generally takes about two weeks. If you have some very deep issues, the process takes as long as it takes. I know that is a vague description, but it is an honest one. You are the only person who truly knows when you feel complete inside with your deeper issues. For many people, the process happens in cycles. By this I mean that you will do a lot of writing and then feel pretty complete and quiet inside. Then something happens in your daily life and an old core issue resurfaces, and it is time to do the writing and tearing or burning exercise again.

This takes us to the maintenance phase. This phase is a lot like brushing and flossing your teeth. If you brush and floss regularly, your visits to the dentist can be relatively pain-free experiences. Keeping our inner environment clean is an ongoing process. If you write and tear or burn regularly, you can stay pretty balanced in your life. You have space inside to respond to issues rather than react. For example, on a scale of 1 to 10, if something happens that is relatively minor—let's say a 2 or a 3—and you respond with a 2 level of intensity, then all is well inside. You are responding appropriately to your environment, and you are able to give a response that is effective. If, however, you respond with a 9 level of intensity, you could say and do things you really do not mean to do or say, and rather than being effective, your communication can be destructive. When you respond to this type of situation with a 9 level of intensity, you are what I call full. You have some unexpressed anger or hurt inside. You might know what it is about, but you might not know there is stuff brewing until you respond with a 9 level of intensity. This type of response is your biofeedback mechanism telling you to do the writing and tearing or burning exercise. Fortunately, or unfortunately, this is an ongoing process, meaning it isn't something you can do just one or twice and be done with it. It is something that you get to use and do through time as you move through your life.

We do not have to wait for a major blowup to remind us to do this inner work. We can use other situations in our lives to "wake us up." I look at how I respond to traffic as my ongoing biofeedback mechanism. If someone cuts me off in traffic and I peacefully allow them to go ahead of me, I know I am current with my emotional state. If, however, I want to ram them with my car, I know I have some things stirring inside that I need to address. The key point here is that you do not need to wait until you are ready to explode before you do your writing and tearing or burning exercise.

WRITING A LOVE LETTER

Some people like the free-form writing style in which they can just jump around without any limitations or restrictions. Others feel intimidated by this type of freedom or feel overwhelmed by the process. For the latter type, there is what I call the Love Letter. Below you will find the form to follow for the Love Letter. You start with the first section and move through until you finish with the sixth section. It allows you to express all of the feelings you might be having about one issue or person. As I stated above, because you are a multidimensional being, you are capable of having many emotions, some of them contradictory, at the same time. The Love Letter gives you a form to express all parts of you in a very complete manner.

You can write the Love Letter many ways. You can write one sentence for each phrase, a paragraph, or a whole page. Write whatever is appropriate or what feels complete at the moment. You can also do it orally. Reading each phrase and completing the sentence silently, or out loud to yourself or to a friend, is also very effective.

Think of a situation that has been disturbing you, and begin writing by completing the first sentence. Continue until you are complete. As you go through the process of writing the Love Letter and get to the last section, do not continue if writing or stating these words feels like a lie; instead, go back to the first section and do it again. At some point, you will be able to finish the entire letter. This is not something you will be mailing or sharing with anyone, so feel free to be as expressive and as honest as you can. After you have written the Love Letter, tear it up or burn it, and then hold on to your basic self or inner child as before and say the same affirmation: "(Your name), I am loving you. I am loving you, (Your name)."

1.   ANGER AND BLAME

I hate it when…

I don't like it when…

I'm fed up with…

2. HURT AND SADNESS

I feel sad when…

I feel hurt because…

I feel awful because…

I feel disappointed because…

3. FEAR AND INSECURITY

I'm afraid that…

I feel scared because…

4. GUILT AND RESPONSIBILITY

I'm sorry that…

I'm sorry for…

I didn't mean to…

I feel guilty for…

5. INTENTION

I want…

I need…

I choose…

6. LOVE, FORGIVING, AND UNDERSTANDING

I love you because…

I love you when…

I thank you for…

I understand that…

I forgive myself for…

AN EXAMPLE

1. I hate it when … you yell at me and make me feel stupid

   I don't like it when … you look at me with disgust

   I'm fed up with … your judgments and your superior attitude

2. I feel hurt when … you ignore my needs and only think of yourself or think you know best

   I feel hurt because … you never ask me what I want or what I feel

   I feel awful because … I want you to honor and respect me and love me for who I am

   I feel disappointed because … I don't know if you will ever see the real me or respect me

3. I'm afraid that … life with you will always be a struggle of wills

   I feel scared because … I don't know how to talk to you anymore

4. I'm sorry that … I am not what you want me to be

   I'm sorry for … all the mean things I've said to you

   I didn't mean to … forget to pay that parking ticket

   I feel guilty for … creating stress in our lives and not doing more

5. I want … us to talk more and to listen more and to understand each other

   I need … for you to be patient with me and to speak with kind words

   I choose … to be more honest with you and not withhold my thoughts and feelings

6. I love you because ... you can be very thoughtful and loving

    I love you when ... you listen to me with understanding and compassion

    I thank you for ... all the times we have laughed and held each other

    I understand that ... you are not perfect and we both have a lot to learn

    I forgive myself for ... holding onto my position and for being thoughtless

EIGHTEEN QUESTIONS TO HELP YOU EXPLORE ANGER AND HURT FEELINGS, OR HOW DID I LEARN TO EXPRESS ANGER AND HURT LIKE I DO?

Take a moment to answer the questions below. Write them down and discuss them with someone you feel is a safe confidant. By doing this, you will learn a lot about who you are and how you have been trained by your caregivers. This exercise might be frightening and might stir some deep emotions. If this is the case, this is an excellent time to do the writing, tearing or burning, and holding on exercise. As you explore, keep asking the questions, "What did I want?" and "What do I want now?" By the way, this is <u>not</u> the time to be sharing your anger and hurt with your caregivers. That will come later. There is more to do and learn before you put yourself in that situation. Be patient as you go through this process.

1. When you were a child, how did your mother express anger at your father?

2. How did your father express anger at your mother?

3. What triggered their anger? How did they react to each other's expressions of anger?

4. Were the basic feelings between them warm and caring or disinterested, hostile, or disapproving?

5. How did your mother/father express anger at you?

6. What would trigger your mother's/father's anger? How did you respond to it?

7. How were you punished for being bad?

8. As a child, did you feel you were being "justly" punished?

9. As an adult, do you feel the punishment was just or unjust?

10. What was considered "bad" in your family?

11. As an adult, do you feel these same things are "bad"?

12. When you were little, did you feel loved? Merely tolerated? Disapproved of?

13. What did your parents do (or not do) to make you feel this way?

14. What made you angry as a child? How did you express your feelings?

15. Was your anger accepted? Ignored? Disapproved of?

16. Do you see any similarity between the way you handled your anger when you were little and the way you handle it now?

17. Do you see any similarity between the way your parents dealt with their anger and the way you deal with yours now?

18. Did you grow up with the feeling that anger was OK? Not OK? Very bad? How do you feel about it now?

A PROCESS ON ANGER OR HURT FEELINGS

The series of questions below gives you another look at how to handle anger or hurt feelings. By looking back at a situation where things might have gotten out of control, you can often learn and grow, thus creating a new pattern in the future. The first step to change will always be awareness. Being aware of your process and how you learned how to deal with issues can give you insight into how to change old habitual patterns.

1. Recall a time when you were angry or hurt. Select one that is still vivid in your memory.

2. What happened? Start from the very beginning of the incident.

3. What were you angry or hurt about?

4. What happened that you feel should or should not have occurred?

5. What expectations, rules, or beliefs were broken or not followed?

6. Who taught you these expectations, rules, or beliefs?

7. Has this type of situation made you angry or hurt before? What patterns do you see?

8. What was the outcome of the interaction?

9. How were you responsible for this outcome?

10. What alternative responses were available to you?

11. How would these alternative responses have changed the outcome?

12. What new expectations, rules, or beliefs would you need to have in order to respond differently than you did in this situation?

13. What can you learn from the situation? Is this a weak spot for you?

14. Move on. Each moment is a new opportunity to experience the bliss of life. Get present.

15. Breathe. State what you are grateful for.

AN EXAMPLE —
THE PARKING LOT EPISODE

When I was going to night school years ago, I would arrive on campus after work a bit harried from my workday and sometimes right on the edge of being late for class. The school had various parking lots, and they were often full. The unwritten rule was to stop your car at the end of an aisle and wait for someone to back out of a space; then you could pull in and park your car in the empty space. The first one to be in the aisle got the first available space. This process worked extremely well until one day, when I was waiting for a space, a car backed out toward me, leaving a space available for me to pull in. However, another driver coming from the opposite direction skipped her turn and pulled into my space ... my space! I was enraged. She broke the rules. She took my space! She should have been polite. She should have followed the rules. She was bad and rude. She didn't honor me. "Doesn't she know who I am? Doesn't she know I have a class to get to?" I learned these rules from my mom, my dad, and my first-grade teacher. I was taught you don't break into lines, you follow the rules, and you are to be respectful to others. We are not animals. We are conscious social beings, and we are to follow the rules so we can live together in peace and harmony. And yes, this type of situation has happened to me before. I see people breaking the rules all the time. I see people shoving and pushing and not respecting other people's space and rights. I often become indignant and feel I need to right the wrong.

In the parking lot situation, I got out of my car, and I yelled and screamed like a madman. I was obviously out of control. The driver of the car rolled up the windows and sat with a look of horror and terror. I continued to scream until I was hoarse. She was not moving her car, nor was she getting out of her car. Eventually, I got back into my car and realized another space had opened up. I pulled my car into the empty space and parked. On my way to class, I yelled a few more phrases of rage at the petrified driver. I arrived to class on time. It took me a long time to calm myself enough to listen to the lecture that night.

I was responsible for my rage because I assumed everyone knew the unwritten parking lot rules. I could have just let the driver have the space, knowing other spaces always become available. I could have then approached the driver in a peaceful manner and brought the unwritten parking lot rules to her attention. If I had handled the situation this way, I could have felt good about being generous, demonstrating to myself that this is an abundant universe. I could have had a smile inside myself for doing a kind deed, and I could have educated an unaware person of the unwritten parking lot rules. If I had maintained my peace, I would have been alert and present for my class and could have gained the knowledge from the lecture.

A number of expectations and realizations would have helped me respond in a peaceful manner:

1. Sometimes people are not aware of what they are doing.

2. People aren't doing things against me.

3. The universe is abundant, and I will be provided for.

4. Some people break rules, and I do not need to teach them a lesson; life will do that.

5. People do what they do. It will be fun to watch and see what they do.

6. Life is a classroom, and life brings many tests to see if I have learned my lessons.

CHAPTER 2

Self-Talk

*N*ow that you have an understanding of what we do as humans when we don't get what we want, the next step is to look inside to see how we talk to or treat ourselves. One of the ways to explore this process is to look or listen to self-talk. If you really grasp the meaning of self-talk, you can begin to understand what makes you tick. Very simply, self-talk is what we say to ourselves, and it is how we interpret what others say or do to us. It goes on all the time, whether we are alone or with thousands of people. At times, it is very quiet, but it can also be very loud.

For example, imagine that I say to you, "Wow, you look great! I love seeing you smile like that. You just have a beautiful glow about you." Those are my words to you, but self-talk is what you say to yourself in response to my words. You could say, "Gee, it is so nice to hear you say that. I really appreciate it. It is nice to have someone acknowledge me and recognize how I am feeling. Thanks." Or your self-talk could be, "Check this guy out, will you? He sure has a line. He is just trying to make me feel good. He is trying to control and manipulate me. I am going to stay clear of this Pollyanna, positive-thinking jerk."

The same words are received totally differently depending on your self-talk. It does not matter what I say to you or what anybody else says to you that counts; it's what you say to yourself. A woman could say to her husband, "I love you," and he could interpret that as "something is up" because he just does not see himself as being worthy of that kind of loving, and there is nothing she can say or do to convince him otherwise.

Our self-talk determines how we look at the world. There is an old saying that applies here: "When a pickpocket sees a saint, all he sees are pockets." It goes the other way as well: "When a saint sees a pickpocket, all he sees is a child of God."

Another concept that describes this is the idea of the self-fulfilling prophecy. We get what we expect we will get. There has been a tremendous amount of research on this subject. The most classic case involved two groups of students. One group was considered exceptional students who were expected to excel beyond the norm. The other group of students was seen as troublemakers, and they were expected to perform below the norm. As in any good test, everything got mixed up and nobody knew which group was which, except the testers, of course.

The teachers were told that the exceptional students were the troublemakers and that the troublemakers were the exceptional students. They were also told that the trouble makers, really the exceptional students, were spoiled and could not conform and that the teachers were not to expect too much from these students except rowdy behavior. The teachers were then told that the exceptional students, really the troublemakers, were very sensitive, creative students and that they demanded a lot of individual time and attention in order for them to perform at their optimum level. Well, as it turned out, the teachers saw what they were told to see. The troublemakers, seen as exceptional students, performed exceptionally well. And the exceptional students, seen as trouble makers, were just that—hard to control, low achievers.

We perform the way we think we should perform. We fulfill our own prophecies. We see the world the way we think we are to perceive it, the way we constantly tell ourselves to perceive it through our self-talk. If we have negative self-talk, we see the world as a very negative place. If we have positive self-talk, we see the world as a very positive place.

"OK, I hear you. Prove it," you say. OK. I accept your challenge.

Stand up and walk outside. Once you are outside, take a deep breath and look around. Notice all the things that are blue. Close your eyes. Now this will be a trick. You need to read and close your eyes at the same time. I want you to remember where all the green was. Open your eyes and notice what you missed. Interesting, huh?

We see what we tell ourselves to see. We get what we focus on or what we expect to get.

What is your self-talk? What is your self-fulfilling prophecy? What has been your self-talk as you read through this section? What did you just say to yourself? Start listening to those thoughts. The first step to change is awareness, so at this point, just start being aware of what you say to yourself. This can be a challenging process. Most of us have never been taught how to be aware of our thoughts. It is like watching yourself wash your face. Most people just wash their faces and grab a towel to dry off. It's about that simple; however, if we are not washing our faces in an effective way, we just might leave that dash of mustard on our cheeks behind. Watching your thoughts is like watching yourself wash your face with awareness.

Years ago when I was a child, I read a story that exemplifies the concept of self-talk. The story was about two men who were going to rob a house. One man was the brains, and the other was the muscle. The smart crook told his buddy to put on a policeman's uniform and stand guard so he could rob a house. The big muscle guy agreed and put on this clean, pressed policeman's uniform with a shiny badge and all. He stood on the corner proud and powerful. While standing there, a little girl walked by and asked for directions. The big muscle guy became soft and kindly and directed her on her way. Shortly after that, a little lady needed help to cross the street safely. The big muscle guy puffed up his chest and gallantly helped the old woman cross safely. Numerous other events occurred, and he began to take pride in his new position in the community as a police officer. About this time, his partner came out of the house he had just robbed with all kinds of goodies. The big muscle guy, seeing a house being robbed, grabbed his partner and arrested him.

His self-talk had changed. He no longer saw him self as a burglar; he saw himself as a policeman, as did others around him. He was to serve and protect. That is who he became. His actions changed because his self-talk changed. How we see ourselves, or how we label ourselves, affects the way others see us, and it also affects the way we interact in the world.

EXERCISES

1. Make a list of your self-talk for the next two minutes.

2. Make a list of what you expect will occur today.

3. Make a list of some of the negative messages you received as a child from Mom, Dad, your primary caregiver, your teachers, and your friends.

4. Make a list of qualities you want to think and feel about yourself. I don't want you to do anything with your list at this point except to just be aware of what you are saying to yourself. Remember, awareness is the first step to change. I just want you to be aware. We will explore how to change your self-talk later. Right now, just be aware and take note.

I AM BAD. NO! I AM GOOD!

How do you really think about yourself? Are you bad, or are you good?

Most of us go around thinking we are bad. We make mistakes all the time. We don't do what we say we are going to do. We lie, we cheat, we behave rudely, we judge others, we steal, we worship false gods, we think of ourselves first instead of others. In short, we break most of the Ten Commandments and the golden rules most of the time. Therefore, we are bad. We do feel a little guilty when we break these rules, so that suggests we have some goodness in us. However, we are still bad. We have ample proof. Look back over the years, and you will see how bad you have been.

Do bad people have loving relationships? Do bad people have jobs that are fulfilling and worthwhile? Do bad people deserve a break today? No, of course not. All of these wonderful things are reserved for good people. They are reserved for people who obey the law and are trustworthy and kind. If your self-talk is that you are bad, how can you have good things? If you "luck" into a good relationship or a good job, you will have to sabotage it somehow because you are bad, and bad people do not deserve good things. Good things are for good people. Bad things are for bad people.

If all of this is true, then it is important to change your self-talk from "I am bad" to "I am good" in order for you to receive good things in your life. Before we explore how to change this core belief, let us look at how we came to believe that we are bad.

We do not have to look too far or too hard to find the source of this belief. All we have to do is look at what has traditionally been called the "terrible twos." Just so you are clear, I do not believe that any of us were terrible when we were two. We were just very curious about our world, and we wanted to touch everything and see how it worked. We used all of our senses, including our mouths. If we got something in our hands, it went into our mouths. We were intent on learning who we were from the moment our eyes opened until the moment we drifted off to sleep. We were exploring and defining boundaries and everything and everyone. Because of our intense learning curve, we exhausted our caregivers. We began saying, "No!" We dropped things, and they broke. We bit people, and they cried. We wet our pants, and we made a mess in the store. We screamed when we were put to bed if we were not tired. We screamed because we were tired. We screamed when we wanted some candy before lunch. We wiggled when we were waiting for some event. We left our toys on the living room floor because we had to go to the bathroom, and we forgot about them because we decided to play motorboat in the toilet. We touched ourselves in places that were naughty. We pulled people's hair. Our parents said, "You are a bad little boy/girl!" We were told we were mean, stupid, selfish, ugly, and terrible.

Our parents, our God at the time, repeatedly told us that we were bad. If God tells us that we are bad, then we must be bad. In time we began to believe that we were bad. Once we believed we were bad, we had to do bad things to show how bad we were. We had to make God right. The cycle of being told we were bad and doing bad things repeated itself over and over. The pattern was set, and for most of us there is no way out. We believe we are bad, and therefore we are.

How to change this pattern is the question. Just by reading this information, we reach a point of awareness. We can start changing our self-talk from "I am bad" to "I am good." The first step to change is awareness. We will look at how to effectively change our negative self-talk on page 43.

POSITIVE SELF-TALK

There is an aphorism in the field of computers: garbage in, garbage out. The way we think about ourselves is based upon how we have been talked to or how we have been programmed. Most of us, as I have suggested, have received a lot of negative programming; thus we think negatively. If we are to think positive thoughts, then we need to program positive thoughts into our computers—our brains.

Below is a list of positive affirmations that you can use to help create positive self-talk. Some of the positive statements will feel great, while others may be too much right now. For some of us, the idea of changing our core beliefs or our self-talk is a foreign concept. For others, it will seem like an obvious next step. As you read through the list, if there are qualities or statements that are not listed that you want to develop within yourself, then add those statements to the list. You can play with this list many ways. You can read the list with a friend, read it to yourself with enthusiasm in a mirror, write the statements on 3 x 5 cards and say them throughout the day, or read one statement every night before you go to bed. Be creative and enjoy the process as you begin reprogramming your computer, your brain, by expanding your positive self-talk.

I am brilliant

I am organized

I am creative

I have a great imagination

I am very smart

I am fine just the way I am

I am happy with the way my body looks

I am energetic

I accomplish what I set out to do

I am successful at what I do

I am very loving

I am deeply loved

I am appreciated

I love in a caring manner

I say and do the "right" things

I am understanding

I am forgiving

I am resourceful

I am a valuable employee

I am unique

I am versatile

I am responsible

I am fantastic

I deliver high-quality work

I am a wonderful mate

I am thoughtful

I am gifted

I am a lot of fun to be with

I love exploring the world

I am willing to share myself

I am adventurous

I am an excellent worker

I am very talented

I inspire others

I am a great person to be with

I am willing to learn

I am good

I am honest

I am a child of God

I am excellent in my own way

I am gentle

I am loving

I am sensitive

I am a center of peace

I am serene

I am successful

I am one with the world

I am one with life

I am aware

I am caring

I am fair

I am open to listen

I am one with God

I am a mature spirit

I am beautiful/handsome

I am intelligent and wise

I am open to growth and
knowledge

I am happy

I can do it

I am a good person

I am generous

I am fun to be with

I am very considerate

I am an excellent student

I am open minded

I am very talented

I am a wonderful human being

I am a good listener

I am smart

I am wonderful

I am a giver

I am good

I am strong

I am wonderful

I am great

I do contribute to my community

I am organized

I am a good lover

I am loved

I do exceptional work

I am wanted

I am talented

I am clever

I am precious

I am fun

I am adorable

I am a good friend

I am nice to talk to

I give good feedback

I am influential

I make life fun

I am respectful

I am fair

I am good at what I do

I am respected in my field

I am a compassionate friend

I have a good sense of humor

I am marriage material

I am a good parent

I have a great body

I have a good mind

I am a team player

I am fair

I have beautiful eyes

I can take good care of myself

I am free

I am independent

I am OK just the way I am

I am rich	I do wonderful things
I am abundant	I am exuberant
I am healthy	I am playful
I am wealthy	I am the way I want to be
I am romantic	I am a good sex partner
I am curious	I am a good provider

THE INNER CHILD

Self-talk to the inner child … what does that mean? Is this another one of those strange things they do in therapy? Who and what is the inner child, anyway?

The inner child is that part of us that seems to be located in our gut. We have all felt it before. Usually when someone is criticizing or attacking us, we feel like we are being hit in our gut with a fist. It seems to be that part of us that responds to scary things. It's the butterfly-in-the-belly idea. The inner child seems to be about five years old or so, and it is capable of expressing great rage, terror, love, fear, and sadness. "Great" is the key word here. It feels emotions in a big way, and we are often consciously or unconsciously controlled by these emotions. Most of us do not like being run by a five-year-old, so we respond to its emotional outbursts with the words we heard from our parents or our care givers. We have, in a sense, internalized our parents' words and methods of discipline.

Most of our parents or caregivers disciplined us with harsh actions or critical words when we did not behave the way they felt we should. They were attempting to train us, or to change our behavior. As time passed, we learned to discipline ourselves. We internalized our parents' method of disciplining, and in time we no longer needed our parents to watch over us or to discipline us. We learned to chastise or punish ourselves. At some point in time, this self-chastisement became an unconscious, automatic process.

Most of us, when we really think about it, know that we are not bad even though we make mistakes and continue to break most of the golden rules. Knowing this, unfortunately, does not seem to be enough to change the pattern.

I believe most of our parents disciplined us the best way they knew how, which was the way their parents disciplined them. Many people today are saying, "I do not want to discipline my kids the way my parents disciplined me. I want to do it differently." This is an admirable intention, but how do we do that? How do we do it differently? What do we say? What do we do?

We need to learn how to discipline ourselves differently. We need to change our self-talk. We need to transform our inner parents. We need to reparent our inner parents. We need to learn how to talk to our inner child with emotionally charged, loving words, with words that inspire and encourage the inner child to create more love, joy, health, and happiness.

Below is a list of statements that the inner child will respond to in a positive way. For some of us, these statements might seem like "airy-fairy" phrases that are lies. If this is your first reaction, then I would suggest that you ask yourself, "How would my mom or dad respond to these phrases? Did they ever say these words to me?" If you never heard this type of talk from your parents, it probably will be challenging for you to believe someone could talk to you with such caring and really mean what they say without some strings attached.

As you read the statements below, notice your reactions. Be aware. Remember to breathe, and read the phrases slowly. Let the meanings sink in. You deserve it.

SELF -TALK TO THE INNER CHILD

I love you.

You are safe.

I'll protect you.

You never have to be alone anymore. I will always be with you.

You are very precious to me.

What do you want from me?

How can I love you?

How are you feeling?

What do you like?

Can I play with you?

What is your opinion? It's very important to me.

I love you just the way you are. You are a good person.

You are perfect to me. I love and accept you.

Everybody makes mistakes.

It's OK that you don't have all the answers.

It's OK if you fail. You can try again. I'll help you succeed. I'm here for you.

I'll never leave you. I will always be here for you.

What can I do to help you?

You can talk to me about anything. I won't judge you. I accept you for who you are.

You're the best. You are good. You are brave. You are courageous. You are talented.

You're a winner. You are appreciated for your talents. You are loving. You are important.

You are special. You are unique. You are everything I want you to be. You are intelligent.

You are loved. You are the best to me. You have a loving spirit. You are thoughtful.

I will always listen to you. Your opinions and feelings matter, and they are important.

We can do it together.

It's all going to work out. You can be and do anything you set your mind to.

You can do what you want, and I will still love you.

I'm sorry if you feel I hurt you.

I'll take better care of you now that I am learning how to love you.

Let's spend some special time together.

I want you to trust me.

I like being with you. You are easy to be with.

I am proud of you. You are wonderful. I think you are very smart.

You can ask me for help.

You don't have to be afraid anymore. We can do it together. I am always here for you.

You look beautiful/handsome with anything you wear.

You are very handsome/beautiful.

Life is a wonderful adventure, and I'm sure we will have many exciting and interesting times together.

You can add to this list other things that are important for you, things that you wish your caregivers had said to you when you were a little child or teenager. We also need to hear these statements and questions from our partners, and our partners need to hear these statements and questions from us.

You ask, "What am I to do with all of these statements and questions?"

Read them to yourself, and/or read them to your partner. Use them to enhance your relationship with yourself and with others. Use them to inspire more comforting and supportive conversations with yourself and others. Some of us had caregivers who installed these types of questions and statements, but some of us did not. If our caregivers were not comforting and nurturing, then it is now our job to comfort and nurture ourselves. The statements and questions above are a beginning step to the process of reparenting ourselves.

SHOULD VERSUS COULD

There are few words that "should" be explained. Or is it "could" be explained? Why am I having a problem figuring out what I should, or is it what I could, say to you?

"Should" is a hot little word that seems to pop up all over the place, especially if you start listening. So, let's look at the word "should" closely and see what it implies and what makes it so challenging.

I remember years ago people corrected me, even scolded me for using the word "should." I really didn't understand why it wasn't a good word to use, and to be honest, I didn't know which word I could use to replace the forbidden "should."

The word "should" implies that you know from a position of total rightness, from God's point of view, how things are to be here on Planet Earth. It implies that you know "right" from "wrong." And if you do not do what you should be doing, then you are wrong and should therefore be severely punished. You should at least feel guilty, a form of self-punishment, for your actions or lack of actions. If you listen for the word "should" in other people's expressions, you will usually hear them using "should" when they haven't done what they should have done or when they have done something that they shouldn't have done.

If you want to have some fun, list all the things that you "should" be doing and all the things you "should not" be doing. After you have your list complete, ask yourself how many of these you have in fact done. You might then ask if the punishment you gave yourself changed your behavior.

Again, what I am suggesting is that the word "should" suggests that we know what is right and wrong, and it also delivers punishment to those who do not do what is right. I am also suggesting that it is not an effective tool to initiate change in ourselves or others.

I would like to look at the concept of "right" and "wrong" for a moment. When I was younger, I believed I knew the difference. As I have grown with time and experience, I now know that I truly do not know the difference between right and wrong. That might sound strange, but bear with me. There are some things that happened to me when I was younger that I knew were wrong. However, now that time has passed and I look back on those experiences, I see just how right those wrongs were. I am not suggesting that you should go out there and hurt people. I am suggesting that I am not able to sit here in judgment of other people's actions or my own actions because I do not know, from God's point of view, what is right or wrong. I am going to let him/her/it/them be the judge of all of that. I figure my job is just to do the best I can in the moment with what I have to work with, and I let other people have that same freedom.

Rather than look to the "rightness" or "wrongness" of a situation, I look to see if it is effective in getting the results I am attempting to accomplish. "Is my method on course with my intention?"

I have found that taking a position of rightness or wrongness is not effective in creating change. Therefore, I have decided not to "should" on myself. There is one more thing that the word "should" does. It limits us. It puts things in a black and white situation. It is either this or that. I personally like a little gray or a little freedom of choice in my life. Having gray in one's life creates challenges, excitement, aliveness, and growth. Life becomes expansive rather than contractive.

There is a neat little word I found that I can use in place of all my old "shoulds." The word is "could." I could wash the dishes after I eat. I could make my bed in the morning. I could be on time. I could be more proactive. I could do things differently than I have in the past. I now have some freedom. I have a choice. If I choose not to wash my dishes or make my bed or be on time, I am also choosing the consequences of those choices. I am not, however, wrong or a bad person. I just have dirty dishes and an unmade bed, and I'm always missing the beginnings of movies. Also, I could at any moment wash my dishes, make my bed, and be on time. I am free to grow and change when I use the word "could." The word "could" gives me choices.

I would encourage you to go back to the list of "shoulds" you made and change all of your "shoulds" to "coulds." You could also work on changing the "shoulds" that come out of your mouth to "coulds." It "could" be fun.

NEEDS

I am sure you have heard yourself or someone say, "I need to do that," or "I need her/him," or "I need it," or "I need to change." These are very powerful statements. They can really set us up for some major emotional pain. The word "need" has a very specific definition. It means that if we do not get what we need, we will die. There are truly only five things that we actually need on Planet Earth: air, food, water, shelter, and loving. The loving that I am speaking of is not romantic love, but rather loving on a larger or humanistic level. We cannot survive very long without these five things. If we don't get enough clean air with oxygen, we will suffocate. If we don't get enough food, we will starve to death. If we don't drink enough water, we will become dehydrated, our kidneys will fail, and we will die. If we don't have the proper shelter to protect us from nature, we can freeze to death or die from overexposure to extreme heat. If we don't get enough loving and touching, we will die. We need these things. Everything else, however, is a "want."

You could say, "I need a house. It's shelter." True, a house is a type of shelter; however, a cardboard shanty can also be an effective shelter. Therefore, you might "want" a house; you do not, however, "need" a house.

Is all this just word games? you ask. The answer is both yes and no. As adults, we are aware that we can survive at different levels with different types of shelters. You could say that when you state that you "need" a house, you know that you really mean that you "want" a house, and so what's the big deal?

Good question. As adults, most of us do in fact understand that. However, there is a part of us—which I call the basic self, the child within, the inner knower, or the subconscious—that does not have discernment. It hears these words and responds as if we truly mean what we say.

For example, if I say, "I need that house," my little basic self hears that and says, "Oh, my God! We have to have that house! If we don't get that house we will die! How can we get it? Hurry! Help! I am scared! This is serious! That house—I have to have it! I don't know how to get it. But I must get it or I will die!" Panic strikes and all the physiological responses for survival start happening. The fight or flight syndrome occurs because you "need" that house. Anxiety kicks in, your blood pressure rises, your stomach shuts down, your blood vessels constrict, and you are ready to battle in order to get that house. If you are not successful, you will die because you "need" that house.

Another approach is to say, "I want that house" or "I choose that house." The message is received as a preference. The little basic self gets into a brainstorming modality and begins to creatively think of all the ways that it could bring that house into your possession. An expansive and determined feeling develops inside as different methods and approaches are explored to give you what you want. A creative process begins: practical solutions and simple action steps start showing up. The process can be fun and exciting instead of fearful and anxious.

Again, I would ask you to be a scientist with this. Watch what happens inside of you when you say you need something and notice the difference when you say you want something. I would encourage you to be very careful with the words you use. List some of those things that you want more of in your life. Look at the list very carefully and ask the question, "Will I die if I do not get this?" If the answer is no, then that item is in fact a want, and you have labeled it correctly.

FIVE STEPS TO CHANGE

Now you are aware of your negative self-talk and some words that can create some emotional pain, and you want to change how you speak to yourself. Great! How do you change in an effective, loving way? That is the question.

Most of us do not know how. We attempt to change a dysfunctional behavior with a dysfunctional method and wonder why things just are not working. We wonder why we are still in emotional pain.

There is an old saying that fits here: "It's not the issue that is the issue; it's how you deal with the issue that's the issue."

I am going to share a process that is effective and loving. It is not the only process that works; however, it is one of the methods I would encourage you to check out and explore for a while. Again, I am encouraging you to be a scientist so you can see and know if this works for you. Once you know how to work these five steps to change, you can use them to change any behavior or pattern in your life.

The first step is called **Awareness.** As I said earlier, you cannot make any changes until you have an awareness that something is going on. Once you have awareness, you can choose to change your behavior. It is at this point that change is possible.

What most people do at this point is slap themselves, figuratively, with negative self-talk as a way of getting themselves to change. They use punishment as a tool to correct their behavior. What happens here is the inner child or basic self says, "Ouch. I see you don't want to be aware of this so I will just keep it secret." So, the negative self-talk continues, but we are not aware of it. It is just looping in the unconscious, running us without our knowing. This is an ineffective approach. We want to be conscious or aware. We want to parent or discipline ourselves differently than our parents disciplined us. Therefore, let's choose another approach.

Rather than punishing ourselves when we hear our negative self-talk, we need to **Acknowledge** that we are aware of our negative self-talk. Because we cannot change until we have awareness, it is important to thank ourselves for allowing the awareness to come to the conscious level. The more conscious and aware you are that you are doing something you wish to change, the more opportunities you have to change. There is an affirmation that goes with this step: "Thank you, (Your name), for letting me be aware of … " This could sound like, "Thank you, Robert, for letting me be aware that I'm beating myself up with negative self-talk."

Your inner child or basic self asks, "Oh, you want to be aware of your negative self-talk?" And you say, "Yes!" And it says, "OK, here it is here, and here, and here." A "popcorn effect" happens: you begin to see your negative self-talk all over the place. This is wonderful because each time you are aware of your negative self-talk, you have an opportunity for change to occur. You say, "Oh boy, more fun. Change is happening."

This brings us to the next step, called **Acceptance.** Rather than beating yourself up for repeating a behavior you wish to change, the more effective and loving method to affect change is to give yourself a reward for moving toward your stated goal. The affirmation for this step is "I forgive myself for …" and/or "I forgive myself for judging myself for …" This could sound like, "I forgive myself for being angry and saying things I really do not mean. I forgive myself for judging myself for being angry and losing control."

We are motivated to move away from pain and to move toward pleasure. Most of us have been trained with the pain model.

To explain this further, let's look at an experiment. I have two little mice. The goal is to get the mice to cross a finish line. I give the first mouse an electrical shock every time is doesn't move toward the finish line. It jumps around and eventually crosses the finish line. Success! I give the second mouse a pellet every time it moves toward the finish line. It runs around and eventually crosses the finish line. Success! Both eventually were successful. However, the first mouse is neurotic and skittish because it is motivated by pain and punishment. The second mouse is contented and peaceful because it is motivated through loving and nourishment. Most of us have been motivated with the electrical shock treatment. That is that slap we give ourselves when we are aware of our negative self-talk or behavior— an ineffective approach.

When I became aware of this process, I wondered why we, as humans, use this electrical shock treatment on ourselves and each other rather than the pellet method. You see it everywhere, in our school systems and in our society at large. In fact, we actually electrocute some people who are really "bad." What I discovered is just a basic fact about animals, and that is we respond faster to pain than we do to pleasure. It is an old survival technique that seems to be programmed in our DNA. I believe, as conscious beings, we can choose to modify or change our behavior in a more effective and loving manner.

OK. So I am not going to punish myself for having negative self-talk. I am going to thank myself for the awareness, and then I am going to forgive myself for slipping into an old pattern. This takes us to the next step, called

Alternative. This is where we have the opportunity to brainstorm and use our imagination to creatively create new behaviors to replace the behavior we are attempting to change. The affirmation for this step is, "Next time, I will do better."

There are two parts to this affirmation. The first part—"Next time"—suggests that I have had this pattern for some time now and it is well ingrained into my consciousness. It's habitual at this point: I will probably do it again. I am in a loving way programming myself how I want to be in the future. The second part is the command to myself: "I will do better."

We seem to be programmed in an interesting way. We usually only hear the last two or three words that are stated. For example, realize what happens when you say, "Don't think of your shoes. Don't think of your fingernails. Don't think about your underwear." Did you think of your underwear? When we tell our child, "Don't drop that glass," s/he hears, "Drop that glass." Or we say, "Don't do that!" and s/he hears, "Do that!" And they do. Or we tell ourselves, "Oh, I feel really bad." And we feel really bad. It just seems to work that way. Interesting, huh? We get what we focus us. Again, this is an ineffective approach.

What I am suggesting we say is, "I'll do better." And our little inner child or basic self hears that and it says, "OK. I'll do better." It hears, "Do better." As simple as this sounds, I want you to know that this is a dramatic change. It's a breath of fresh air. I'm not being beaten for making a mistake. I am being encouraged to do better. My inner child or basic self says, "Yes, thank you. I can do that."

It is at this point that we can do some brainstorming and use our creative imagination. We ask ourselves, "OK, if I were to do better, what would that look like? What would that sound like?" We can think about how we could have done it better or differently. This is a great place for the techniques of writing, tearing or burning, placing your hands on your abdomen and saying positive affirmations, or using some of those statements or questions to the inner child identified in Chapter 2. There are a lot of alternative things we could do. As you go through this book, you will learn more alternative methods.

Now that you have come up with a list of new and more effective alternatives, we move to the fifth and last step called **Action**. This is the step where you can choose to do one or all of the alternatives that you thought of in step four. You don't have to do everything right now. You are in a process of change. Be gentle with yourself. Enjoy the process. Remember, it's not the issue that is the issue; it's how you deal with the issue that's the issue.

The five steps to change can be a fast, effective method for change. You just need to remember three short affirmations: "Thank you, (Your name). I forgive myself for (insert thought/feeling/action). Next time, I'll do better."

You might be driving down the road and all of a sudden you are aware that you are in your negative self-talk pattern. "Oh, awareness! Thank you for letting me be aware that I'm beating myself up. I forgive myself for being so critical of myself. Next time, I'll do better. I think I will just say, 'Robert, I am loving you. I am loving you, Robert' for about three minutes." Then about seven minutes down the road, you are again aware that you are in your negative self-talk pattern. "Oh, awareness. Thank you for letting me be aware that I am in my negative self-talk pattern. I forgive myself. Next time, I will do better. Let's see, I think I will say some positive affirmations." Seven minutes down the road, "Oh, awareness." Now, you have a habitual loop that will set you free. The more you go through these five steps, the faster you will create the desired behavior.

AN EXAMPLE

A while back, I was working with a Rolfer, a type of body worker, to deal with a chronic, nagging, low back pain that I had not been able to resolve. After a few sessions, she indicated that I locked my knees when I stood up. "Of course I do," I thought. "Doesn't everyone? Isn't that the way you are supposed to stand up?" She patiently explained to me that by locking my knees, I was pushing my hips forward, thus putting my body out of alignment, which was one of the reasons I had lower back pain. She demonstrated the "correct" way of standing with my thighs engaged and my knees unlocked. "Great," I thought. "I will just stand the way she described and everything will be just fine."

Unfortunately, it was not that simple. I discovered that as soon as I became unconscious about my knees, I would lock them. I decided to apply the five steps to change concept to help me change a deeply ingrained, unconscious habit. Whenever I became aware of my knees being locked, I thanked myself for the awareness, I forgave myself for any judgments I had for continuing to maintain a behavior that was causing me physical pain, and then I said, "Next time, I'll do better." I took a breath and unlocked my knees, and I moved on. This little process of knee locking went on for a long time. Then one day, I became aware that my knees were not locked. Wow! What a wonderful discovery. I thanked myself for the awareness, and I gave myself words of appreciation by saying, "Good job!" I would like to say that from that point forward, I always caught myself with my knees unlocked, but that would not be the truth. I can say that I slowly, ever so slowly, became more and more aware that I had knees and that there was a better approach to standing. In time, I was able to establish a new, unconscious, habitual pattern of standing with my knees unlocked. I also discovered that this new pattern of unlocked knees disappeared when I was tired.

I discovered that changing old, habituated patterns requires constant focus and attention. It doesn't matter if I am changing my negative self-talk; an addiction to cigarettes, alcohol, or food; or locked knees. The process is very much the same. I also discovered that I can change these patterns by using the five steps to change.

CHAPTER 3

What Keeps Us Stuck

THE ICEBERG CONCEPT

*E*arlier I suggested that the first point of change is awareness and that we cannot change anything until we are aware of it. I also suggested that it is our unconscious that runs us. In order for us to change, we need to be aware of how we allow our unconscious thoughts and actions to become conscious. In order to understand this concept better, I want you to look at the picture of the iceberg below.

Besides being amazing and beautiful, it also demonstrates this concept of awareness. As you look at the picture, notice how much of the iceberg is actually below the surface of the water and how little is being revealed. The portion that is below the surface is our unconscious. I am suggesting that this is what runs us. This is what was put in from the moment of conception, and through every waking and sleeping moment, right up to this very moment. Stuff is going into our unconscious all the time. We are not aware of it: Stuff, just keeps going in. It is being sorted and stored for some use later. Become aware of the support you are sitting on. Be aware of your body pressing against the object. After a few moments you won't need to be aware of it. Your mind will quiet, and it will disappear from your conscious awareness. Your mind/body will just put the information away somewhere for some future reference. It goes into the unconscious.

The point I am attempting to make is threefold. First, your unconscious is huge. It is full of a lot of data that you no longer need in the moment. However, it is there, and it helps you to quickly discern if you are safe or not. It helps you to discern if what you are doing is the "right" thing or the "wrong" thing. Second, your conscious self is very limited. It is what you think you believe. It is what you think controls your world. Third, your point of awareness is even smaller. It is always changing depending on what is going on in the moment.

AUTOMATIC PILOT

I'm sure you have wondered why you keep doing the same things over and over again, knowing full well that what you are doing just does not work, but you just keep doing it anyway. Right?

"Why?" you ask.

Well, one answer to this question is simply, "You are on automatic pilot." Automatic pilot? What do you mean? Who set it?

I'd like to tell you a little story that will help to explain. Let's say you live in California and you want to sail a ship to Hawaii. You know where you are going. You know the direction you need to go in order to get there. So you begin to build a ship. As you build your ship, you have a special little device that you can set, and it will take the ship wherever you want it to go. Knowing Hawaii is southwest from where you are, you set your special device, your automatic pilot, for southwest. Everything is set. You finish building your boat, and everything is in working order. You start on your trip to Hawaii. You are sailing along, enjoying the sun. Your automatic pilot is working like a charm, and you are well on your way. You close your eyes. Visions of Hawaii dance in your mind. At some point you open your eyes and discover that your ship is heading straight for an island. With terror in your heart, you grab the helm and point the ship away from the island. Feeling comfortable again, you settle back and close your eyes. Now, while you are off dreaming, your automatic pilot comes back into control and redirects the ship back to the southwest, straight for the island. A seagull cries out. You open your eyes only to discover that you are heading on a collision course with the island. Again, you grab the helm and point the ship away from the island. Whew!

Our automatic pilot will always move us in the direction that it has been set. So, who set our automatic pilot? It was set years ago by our parents, our primary caregivers, our siblings, our teachers, our friends, and even ourselves. Sometimes it was set by verbal commands. More often, it was set by what was not said, by nonverbal actions. It was also set by the experiences we have had. Once the automatic pilot is set, it remains set until we consciously go back and change it. One thing that is very interesting about the automatic pilot is that when it is set, we are making the best decisions we can at that moment based on all the information we have to work with. As children, we discovered what we needed to do in order to survive in our environment. We survived. We are still alive. However, what kept us alive in our families of origin probably will not be effective in the world we now find ourselves living in today. As adults, we do not want to carry on and live our lives based on the perceptions of an infant, a young child, or an adolescent.

As you probably are becoming aware, the automatic pilot is in that vast unconscious part of us. Remember the iceberg? Most of us have not gone back inside and changed our automatic pilot. And if we have attempted to change it, we probably used methods we were taught. We can begin to use the five steps to change as a method of changing our automatic pilot. By focusing on positive affirmations and positive self-talk, we can begin to send the automatic pilot new orders and new perceptions from which our ship is to be steered.

What outdated messages are you still following? As a point of awareness, reflect on what beliefs about yourself you would like to let go of and what beliefs you would like to consciously program.

INTENTION VERSUS METHOD

Earlier, I was suggesting that the method of punishment, or the electrical shock treatment, just was not effective. When I was speaking of "right" and "wrong," I put the words in quotation marks, suggesting that the concept of "right" and "wrong" is a subjective concept. Now for some people, once again, I'm walking on very thin ice. They might say, "What do you mean right and wrong is subjective? You don't believe in right or wrong? You're wrong! You're bad! You don't know what you are talking about!"

Do you hear any harsh, critical, punishing statements in there? I do.

I attempt to avoid positions of "right" and "wrong" because they throw me into judgments and I find that when I move into judgments, I lose and everybody else loses. I prefer to view life, actions, and thoughts from the point of view of being effective or ineffective.

In order to explain this further, I want to explore the concept of "intention versus method." It is another one of those major concepts that can change how you walk through your daily life, so you can experience more of the love, joy, peace, and happiness that we, as humans, are all longing for.

Here's a story. We are living in Los Angeles and our goal is to get to San Francisco as quickly as possible. You are going north, and I am going south. The question is: Who gets there first? You might judgingly laugh at me and say, "Buddy, I can't believe you are even talking. Of course I'll get there first. We all know San Francisco is north of Los Angeles. You can't get there by going south."

Yes, San Francisco is north of Los Angeles, and I do look a little silly by going south. However, I forgot to mention that your method of transportation is by foot and that I'm riding on a supersonic jet.

We both get there. Our methods were different. The intention was to arrive as quickly as possible. Is one way "right" or "wrong"? No. One method is just more effective, simply because it's based on speed.

Now, if we change our intention from speed of arrival to who has the most experiences, I would suspect the person walking would have the most experiences. If we change our intention, then the method that is most effective changes. Both methods are effective; neither is "right" or "wrong." The most effective one is based upon our intention.

A friend of mine once told me, "Be as steady as the North Star and as flexible as the wind." That means I keep my eyes on where I am going. I know where I am going—that's my intention. However, it's how I get there, and my method, that keeps changing. I am not attached to the method. I am attached to the end result, my intention. The questions I keep asking are, "Is this working? Is this taking me to where I want to go? Am I getting the results I want? Am I 'on course' or 'off course'?"

ON COURSE – OFF COURSE

How do you know if what you are doing is working? How do you know if you are "on course" or if you are "off course"? These are questions we all seem to ask from time to time. They are important questions, and our universe is giving us the answers all the time. The problem is that most of us do not know how to interpret what our universe is telling us. Some of us don't listen very well, while others seem to be hard of hearing. Apparently, we only respond when we are being yelled at or hit on the head with a club.

When the Apollo spacecraft was sent to the moon, it was off course more than it was on course. When it moved off course, a signal was sent to mission control and a corrective measure was taken. At some point in time, the spacecraft was off course again. Another signal was sent to mission control and another corrective measure was taken. This process continued all the way to the moon—the desired goal.

As we move through our lives, we are in a very similar process. When we are off course, we feel anger, hurt, resentment, depression, anxiety, fear, or jealousy. We feel pain. Pain can be described in many ways. How we describe it is not the real issue here. The real issue is, "Are we listening to the feedback our universe is giving us?" Also, be aware that our universe does not really care how much pain it has to deliver to us in order to get us to move back on course. The longer we ignore something, the more significant the pain. At some point, we become aware of what we are doing. Once aware, we can turn and get back on course. When we are on course, we feel love, joy, health, and happiness.

The more we become aware of who we are and what our needs are, the faster we can respond and keep ourselves on course with less pain. There is an old saying that the path is straight and narrow. It is. Because once we learn how to stay on course, it takes very little pain to get us to turn toward our goal. A key question to ask yourself is, "Am I experiencing love, joy, health, and happiness?" If the answer is yes, then you can pretty much rest assured that you are "on course." If the answer is no, then you can be assured that you are "off course."

Being off course does not necessarily mean that you are in the wrong job or the wrong relationship and that you now have to quit your job or end your relationship. It just might mean that your attitude, or your self-talk, is negative or that you are repeating an old habit or action that no longer serves you. When we feel the effects of being off course, we are being told to change our attitude and our actions. Knowing to listen to the messages your universe sends you, and then responding in an appropriate way, is a key to experiencing love, joy, health, and happiness, or staying "on course."

It is also more empowering to move toward what you want rather than away from what you don't want. By focusing on moving toward love, joy, health, and happiness, you increase your chances of having more of the positive. If you focus on moving away from the negative, then you increase your chances of having more of the negative. Because you have a choice, choose to focus on what you want, and keep taking steps toward your goal.

COMFORT ZONE

You say, "I want to change. Yet, I seem to be doing everything but what I need to do in order to change and make things better for myself. I don't understand."

Another reason we stay stuck in our old behavior patterns can be seen by identifying our *comfort zone.*

The comfort zone can be easily seen by playing with the thermostat in your home. If you set the thermostat at 70 degrees Fahrenheit, it will regulate the temperature and the room will be comfortable. If the temperature drops below 65 degrees, the heat will come on and raise the temperature to 70 degrees. If the temperature rises above 75 degrees, the air conditioner will come on and cool the room down to 70 degrees. The comfort zone would be between 65 degrees and 75 degrees.

We all have our own built-in comfort zones. We have one for money, one for love, one for free time, one for health, and others for just about anything else we care to measure. We have set these comfort zones by our life experiences as young children, as adolescents, and as adults. Our parents, our peers, our society, and our environment have all influenced us and, in their own way, helped us set our comfort zones. Unfortunately, most of the comfort zone setting has been programmed unconsciously. We often are not aware that we are programming our unconscious as we go through our day-to-day activities.

However, the end result of an unconscious process is an automatic thermostat that regulates many aspects of our lives. If we have too much pain or sorrow, we will do whatever it takes to get out of the pain and sorrow. It is outside of our comfort zone. Also, if we have too much love, joy, health, happiness, or abundance, then we will do whatever it takes to get back into our familiar comfort zone where we feel safe and where we know what to expect.

What I am suggesting is that anytime we attempt to change a behavior or to create something new in our life, we are moving outside of our comfort zone and will feel uncomfortable. As crazy as it might sound, we will want to return to where we were before, to our old habits … to our comfort zone.

Part of the process of change is identifying what our current comfort zone is and then redefining it in the direction we want it to go.

"Wait a minute," you say. "I feel uncomfortable all the time about not having enough money to buy the things I want. That's not a comfort zone! I'm uncomfortable, I'm uncomfortable!"

Yes, I hear you're uncomfortable, and I would like to suggest that feeling uncomfortable is part of your comfort zone. Feeling comfortable about money matters would be out of your comfort zone and probably outside of your experience. I would ask you to look at how your parents handled money and how your society handles money. What is the mass media telling you about money? Feeling comfortable about money is a very uncomfortable concept for many people. I do know some people, however, who are very comfortable about money. Yes, some of them do have a lot of money, but some of them do not have much money at all. The amount of money a person has or does not have does not seem to be the issue.

"So what? I don't like this. What do I do with all of this? I'm feeling uncomfortable. I don't like you anymore. This isn't fun. I want to stop. This is too much work. You're changing things around on me. I can't think. I'm confused. I feel overwhelmed. Leave me alone. I want to go to sleep."

OK, let's take a break. There's no need to go get a piece of paper or anything. Just relax and let your mind go and be comfortable, or should I say be uncomfortable. Just do or feel whatever it is that you usually do or feel. Once you are in your comfort zone again, give yourself permission to be uncomfortable as you explore your comfort zones.

Think about how much money you feel comfortable about having. Looking at your checkbook and the balance you've maintained for the past few years will give you a good indication of what your financial comfort zone has been up until now. Look at how much you have in your pocket or purse and in your savings account. Also, look at how much money you owe and to whom you owe it.

In order to determine what your comfort zone is in regard to loving, look at the relationships you have in your life. How much love and joy have you been experiencing over the past few months or years? How close do you let people get to you? How often do you argue or fight with those around your? How often do you touch or say, "I love you"?

I am suggesting that it is important for you to clearly identify what your comfort zones are before you attempt to change them.

If you want to write down your thoughts and feelings about this, that's great. If you would rather just think about it, that's great too. Do whatever you feel comfortable doing, or do whatever you feel uncomfortable doing.

If you want to increase your *comfort zone* so you can receive more love, joy, health, happiness, and abundance, then the five steps to change mentioned earlier can be a wonderful way to create a transformational experience in your life.

Remember that the first step to change is awareness. So being aware of your comfort zone is your first step. Again, look at your checkbook. First, how do you feel about the balance? Let's say you want more money in your account. As you look at that balance, what is your feeling? If it is a negative feeling like fear or anger, go to the second step. Second, thank yourself for being aware of that feeling. Third, forgive yourself for that feeling. In the fourth step, tell yourself, "Next time, I'll do better." The "doing better" is twofold. Initially, we are dealing with the negative feelings, or the reaction to the balance. Later, we will also look at some action steps to actually do something different in the world to create a different result—a higher balance in your checkbook. In the fourth step, do some brainstorming: what are some things you can do to create a different feeling or a different way of dealing with the issue? You could do some writing, tearing and burning; some positive affirmations; nurturing self-talk with the inner child; or move from judgment to acceptance. After you list your various options, do the fifth step, action, and do one or all of your options.

You might be saying, "OK, I got all that, but how do I move from judgment to acceptance?" That's a great question. Let's explore those two emotions and, hopefully, your question will be answered.

JUDGMENT OR EVALUATION

A friend of mine once told me that next to every truth stands a lie, that one person's ceiling is another's floor, and that to follow a truth is like walking a razor's edge—it is easy to fall off in error. I find defining the difference between evaluation and judgment to be in this fine-line category. As I start to define evaluation, I feel myself moving over into judgment, and as I start to describe judgment, I move into evaluation.

So, what is the difference between judgment and evaluation?

Evaluations are positive. Judgments are negative. Evaluations help you decide what you want more of in your life and create a sense of connection. Judgments can create confusion and separate you from others. Evaluations are expansive in nature; judgments are constrictive. Evaluations give you freedom of choice; judgments limit your behavior and the behavior of others. Evaluations merely state what "is" in a neutral, objective manner. Judgments indicate an opinionated, subjective value. Evaluations can be seen as a mental or a scientific approach, and judgments are emotional in nature and often suggest a moral, self-righteous approach.

I would encourage you to reread that paragraph again. Go slow. Challenge it. Process it. What parts ring true to you and what parts stir some deep emotion? Obviously, I am encouraging you to move toward evaluation versus judgment. Challenge that.

"OK, enough comparisons and enough challenges," you say. "What is the difference between judgment and evaluation? I still don't understand. How can I decide if I like something if I don't have an opinion or a judgment about it? How can I judge whether it is good for me or not good for me? I am confused."

This is the razor's edge that I spoke about earlier. Discerning the difference between judgments and evaluations in some areas is very easy, while in other areas it is very tricky. It's something that you just have to play with and watch very closely. Let's look at some examples.

Some statements that are judgmental are these: He is ugly. I think she is stupid. I am such a fool. Can you believe she is wearing that dress? That guy drives like he is half-asleep.

In each of the judgmental statements, the speaker is assuming to know something about something s/he does not truly know anything about, and the statement sounds very opinionated. Notice also that the speaker is placing himself/herself in a superior position. The expressions of compassion and understanding are not present. The general tonality is one of scolding or ridicule. The primary position is I know what is right, and what you are doing, wearing, or saying is wrong!

Some statements that evaluate are these: He is six feet tall, and he weighs 95 pounds. Every time I ask her to do this task, I have to show her all the steps. I find I keep repeating the same pattern over and over again. The red dress she was wearing had nine yellow dots the size of basketballs, placed four inches apart. He drove his car down the freeway at 26 mph. I saw him pour a glass of milk into his gas tank.

In the statements above, notice that descriptions are expressed in detail. The adjectives describe very specific traits. An opinion is not stated, and the speaker is not running assumptions. S/he is just describing what is seen. There is no rightness or wrongness presented. Everything is very factual.

You say, "Well, I don't like red dresses with yellow dots the size of basketballs." That's fine. In fact, it is good that you know what you like to wear and what you dislike. You enter into a judgment, however, when you state, "That dress is ugly, and anyone wearing it is stupid and obviously has no taste!"

And you might respond, "I know style. That's my job, and I know that red dresses with yellow dots are disgusting and anyone wearing them or suggesting someone should wear them is crazy and stupid."

Notice how this position creates separation? Notice the position of self-righteousness? Notice all the assumptions? Who is defining what is ugly and what is stupid? Whose taste of clothing is "right"? The above speaker is assuming s/he knows the "right" answer to all of these questions. Beauty, intelligence, and fashion are all subjective and relative to some arbitrary standard that someone has set.

Judgments indicate a position of self-righteousness. The underlying assumption is that I am right and you are wrong and that you must do what I do and must think like I think. If you don't, well, judgment will be directed at you. Evaluations describe what you see, hear, or feel. They reflect an attempt to discover what works for you and what does not work for you. The underlying foundation is the knowledge and acceptance of what works for me might not work for you and what works for you might not work for me.

For the next week, watch how you describe people, places, and events. Ask yourself if you are evaluating or judging what you are seeing. How do you feel when you accurately describe what you see? How do you feel when you judge what you see? Be aware of how your body reacts. I would also encourage you to listen to how other people describe people, places, and events and watch how you react to their evaluations and judgments. Then you might want to ask yourself which process, evaluating or judging, sets you free and allows you to create more of what you want in your life.

CHAPTER 4

Keys to Getting UnStuck

ACCEPTANCE, ATTITUDE & ALTITUDE

"If judging hurts me and others and evaluation is a more expansive and uplifting process, then how do I stop judging? I have a habit of judging. I only do those things that I think are right, and I only judge those things that I think are wrong. I do know the difference between right and wrong. I try not to do those things that are wrong, and I don't like it when other people do the wrong things. I guess that I don't buy your evaluation argument. I see the value of it, but I think it falls short. You aren't really giving me anything I can use or a way to move out of my judgments. And, as I said, 'I know when I am right, and I know when you are wrong.'"

I hear you. You and everyone else on our planet does what they think is right to get what they want. We're all doing the best that we can with the information we have. If we truly knew better, we would do better. And, you are right. We need to take another step in this process to move out of our judgments. If we are to be truly out of judgment, then we need to accept ourselves and others as we all are … period. That's it! No change is required. We are fine just the way we are.

"Wait a minute," you say. "Now you really have gone off the deep end! I'm reading your book because I want my life to be different. I want the world to be different, and now you're telling me that I'm to accept myself and others for the way we are? You've got to be kidding. My wife/husband/

boyfriend/mom/dad/whomever really needs to change. I don't like my life. I don't like how much money I'm making. I don't like my comfort zone. I don't like my anger. I don't like your ideas or your book. You're crazy!"

This is a good place to do the writing, tearing or burning, and holding on process. Emotions are being stirred. This is good. You are out of your comfort zone. You are in the process of change right now. Stating what you don't like can bring you to a point of awareness. Remember, awareness is the first step to change. Acceptance is the second step. Take a deep breath, and let's explore this concept of acceptance a little deeper.

The process of moving you to acceptance is easy to describe and to understand. However, it can be a challenge to manifest acceptance inside ourselves at times. There are two basic steps in the process of acceptance: we need to change our attitude, and we change our attitude by changing our altitude. Here, let me explain.

Moving out of judgment to acceptance requires an attitude of gratitude. If you can be grateful that something has occurred, is occurring, or will be occurring, then it is easy to accept the event. If you have an attitude of resistance, judgment, or resentment, it can be very difficult to move to a position of acceptance. "That's great," you say. "But how do I move to an attitude of gratitude when I'm angry and I don't like what's happening? I'm not grateful. I'm resentful. I'm angry at them or me for what is happening or for what happened. What happened is wrong. It hurt me or someone else. It's terrible. Be grateful? You have to be kidding."

I couldn't have said it better. When we feel this way, it is very hard to move out of judgment and into acceptance. This is why it is important to move to the next step.

Changing our attitude requires us to change our *altitude*. We have to look at the event from a different point of view. This step is by far the most challenging step to take. It is the place where most of us get stuck. Hopefully, I can give you some keys on how to break free from your positions of rightness and your comfort zone so you can change your altitude, change your attitude, and move from judgment to acceptance.

Let me tell you another fun little story to help make my point. Let's say I'm walking on a trail up a mountain path. I'm having a wonderful time. The birds are singing, there is a breeze in the air, and I'm admiring the beautiful cloud formations. Ouch! I trip and fall, and I sprain my ankle. What a curse! My day is ruined. I'm angry at myself for being so clumsy and twisting my ankle. How do I move to a position of acceptance? Step one: change my attitude to being grateful that I twisted my ankle, which is swelling up as we speak. Great! Have an attitude of gratitude. How do I do that? Move to step two: change my altitude or my viewing point. How? OK, so here I am, looking at that mountain path from the point of view of an eagle flying overhead. As I am sailing on the wind, I look down and see a huge rattlesnake just around the bend, right in the middle of the path. If I had continued at the same pace, I see that I would have walked right into the rattlesnake, and it would have bitten me and I could have died from its poisonous venom. I am now so glad that I twisted my ankle. This was a gift from God. I'm now in a position of acceptance, and I can deal with my situation in a more effective and powerful manner. I am no longer judging myself. I feel grateful for twisting my ankle.

"But how do I know if that snake was really around the bend? Aren't I lying to myself and pretending I know something that I don't?" Yes, possibly you are pretending you know something that you don't really know. I sense we all pretend we know a lot about things we really don't know. The difference here is you are making a very conscious effort to affect a change inside yourself, a change that will give you more freedom and inner peace—qualities we experience when we are in acceptance.

You might say, "OK, I got it, but that's a simple story. What about the really hard things that happen to us in life?"

Challenging things do happen to all of us. Some events are life changing, and I agree that it is these life-changing events that require the most work. Life-changing events are just that … life changing. Remember, it is not the issue that is the issue; it is how we deal with the issue that is the issue. We are now looking at how to deal with issues in an uplifting manner so that no matter what happens, we are more accepting of the experience. We are in the process of learning how to use everything for our upliftment, advancement, and growth. I am not suggesting this is an easy process. That would be a lie. It is a challenge. However, the two primary rewards for working the process are freedom and joy.

In order to change your altitude, it helps to ask questions. Questions are wonderful tools. We can use them to change or to hold our focus in the direction we wish to take our life. Some questions create anxiety and separation, others create depression, and others create a window of fresh air or freedom. Some questions can help us change our altitude, thus changing our attitude and moving us to a position of acceptance.

QUESTIONS

Whenever we ask a question, we set in motion a process of search and find inside ourselves. We create a void that our brain tries to fill. Our brain begins looking through all the memory banks available, through everything we have seen, heard or read. This process continues until an answer is found.

The quality of the answer our brain finds is directly related to the quality of the question that has been asked. I come from the school of thought that we have all of the answers inside ourselves. We just need to ask the right question. If this is true, then the question most often is, "What is the right question?"

Questions that begin with "why" often produce anxious or depressed feelings. "Why did this happen to me?" "Why did they say or do that?"

"Why do people always forget me?" "Why was I singled out?" "Why don't they know better?"

"Why" is also one of those words that imply we have done something wrong. Most of us have a knee-jerk reaction to the question "why"—we immediately move into the defensive. This pattern began when we were little children crawling around on the floor picking up every piece of paper, worm, or nail we could find and sticking it in our mouths. Our moms would panic. As our moms jabbed their fingers into our mouths for the object we were scientifically tasting, they'd be shouting, "Why did you do that?" This scene changed as we grew older, but the "Why did you do that?" remained the same. We learned to defend ourselves against the "why" question at a very early age by declaring our rightness.

The truth is that there really is only one answer to a "why" question. The answer is "because." "Why did you do that?" "Because I did." Be a scientist and check this out. See if what I am suggesting is true. I would encourage you to ask a lot of "why" questions during the next few days and listen very closely to how people answer you. Note the first word they use the next time you ask someone a "why" question. It will always be "because" followed by some excuse or defense.

When we ask "why" questions, our brains go into a search and find process. It knows there really is not an answer, so it tries to give some rational lie that we just might accept. Not getting the answer we want, we ask again and again, sending ourselves into an anxious or depressive loop with no way out and no real answer.

The question I have to ask is, "When you ask someone the 'why' question or someone else asks you the 'why'" question, are you or are they really getting the information that is needed to initiate change in behavior?" I suspect not.

I would suggest you use another word instead of "why" when you want to gather information, initiate change, or change your attitude. The word could be "what," "how," "when," or "where."

The question, "Why did you do that?" could be changed to, "What caused you to do that?" "What did you learn by doing that?" "What did you think you would get by doing that?" "Where did you learn to do that?" "When did you learn to do that?" or "What was the outcome you wanted to have by doing that?"

As you can see, many questions would help you or the other person understand a particular event or behavior. Our attitude can change as a natural consequence. With understanding comes empathy.

Watch your self-talk. Watch for the "why" question, and when you hear yourself asking "why," change the question to "what." Also, listen to your response to the "why" question when someone else asks it. Notice how you move toward the defensive. Ask yourself, "What is it that they are really asking me?" Once you are clear on what is really being asked of you, answer that question in an attempt to create understanding. You will discover that there really is no need to defend your position.

Some other very powerful questions to ask follow:

"What am I learning right now?"

"What did I learn today?"

"How can I use this for my advancement?"

"Where is the humor here?"

"What is great right now?"

"What is special about this moment?"

"What is my next step?"

"What am I choosing to do right now?"

"How would my (hero, mentor, or high self) handle this?"

"How can I let this go?"

"What else do I want to know to make a better decision?"

"Where do I want to go to gather more information?"

"Whom do I want to talk to in order to complete this?"

"What is the good news about this event?"

"How can this strengthen me?"

"What could I have done differently?"

"What am I completing here?"

These questions can set your mind in a direction of finding answers that can set you free. They can focus your brain in a direction that can open doors and move you in a positive direction.

CREATE, PROMOTE, OR ALLOW

Another question that can assist you in the process of moving into a positive direction is, "How did I create, promote, or allow this to happen to me?" This question can assist us in moving out of victim consciousness and into a position of being accountable and responsible for our lives and what we are experiencing in them.

Before we go too far, let me define these terms so you can have another level of understanding of what I am suggesting.

First, let's look at the word "create." Let's say we are in a nice restaurant, having a great time, and I turn to the guy next to me and I say, "Buddy, you're really ugly!" He hears this, and he hits me in the face. "Ouch! Why did you hit me?" It would be hard to be a victim here. It is easy to see how I "created" that experience. I am not suggesting that we deserve to be hit; it's just easy to see the cause and effect in this situation. I can clearly claim responsibility for my actions.

Now, let's look at the word "promote." This is a little subtler. We are at the same restaurant, still having a great time. I'm minding my own business. I'm not saying anything insulting to anyone. However, I say to you, loud enough for my neighbor to hear, "See that guy next to me? He is really ugly!" The guy next to me hears this statement and promptly hits me in the face. "Ouch! What did you hit me for? I was only talking to my friend." I can begin to claim the victim point of view; however, I did promote that incident.

The last word, and the hardest to claim, is "allow." This one can get real sticky, so bear with me. We are at the same restaurant, having an exceptionally great time. I'm behaving myself. I'm not saying anything insulting about anyone. I'm just enjoying your company. However, this guy next to me gets into a fight with another guy. All of a sudden, a chair comes flying and hits me in the head. "Ouch! Why do bad things always happen to me? Why do I always get hit in the head? It's not fair!" I have a great victim story. However, I know when people get into physical fights, people get hurt, and because I decided to stay there, I allowed myself to get hurt.

You say, "But it all happened so fast. I would have moved if I had known something bad was going to happen." Yes, that is true. We all know, however, that in this physical world, our physical bodies bump into things and things bump into our physical bodies. So we could isolate ourselves and stay safe, but we would probably get very bored. In order to experience and express our freedom, we go out into the world. We drive down freeways at 65 mph in little metal boxes on wheels, pretending that we are safe. We all know that isn't true. However, we get in those things every day. I am suggesting that we are placing ourselves in a place where we are allowing ourselves to get hurt all the time. It is a choice. It is not always a conscious choice, but when you look, you will see that at some point you made a choice.

"What about young children who are physically or emotionally abused? Did they make a choice? Are they responsible for their abuse?"

This is where it gets sticky, and I am not going to pretend that I have all the answers to this type of question. I can apply the acceptance model to this type of situation, however. Some of our most creative and talented role models have had to walk through horrible childhood experiences, and it is often these horrible experiences that have made them the giants that they are. I am not proposing abuse on any level. I am just acknowledging that it exists, and in order for us to use it for our upliftment, advancement, and growth, we often have to move out of the victim position. I guess the primary choice is the choice to be born. If that is a choice we made, then by choosing to be born on this planet at this time, we are allowing ourselves to experience bumps and grinds on the physical level.

This could take us into a religious or spiritual discussion; however, this is not where I want to take this book. I would ultimately encourage people to go inside themselves, discover their own truth here, and consult with their own religious or spiritual directives. Sometimes, in order to see things from a position that allows us to move to an attitude of gratitude, we do need to look at things from a higher religious or spiritual point of view.

There is another point I would like to make in regard to being accountable and responsible for our lives and what happens to us. There is a story that many years ago, someone approached Sigmund Freud while he was smoking a cigar. They asked, "Hey, Sigmund. What's that phallic symbol you are sucking on? What does that mean?" And his response was, "Sometimes a cigar is just a cigar." We go through life trying to figure out how we created, promoted, or allowed something to happen to us, but sometimes "poop happens." Sometimes bad things do happen to good people for no other reason than they were just there. They were born and ...

There is no training, supplement, or "miracle pill" that can make us immune to adversity. In fact, it might be wise to expect adversity as an inevitable part of life. It's not a matter of if it comes your way; it's a matter of when and how severely it strikes your life. I believe we all get to deal with something challenging as we go through this life. I don't care how much money you have, how beautiful or handsome you are, or how smart you are. We will all get to deal with some adversity sooner or later.

Remember, it's not the issue that is the issue; it's how you deal with the issue that's the issue.

It is helpful to accept that ill fortune or adversity is an inevitable part of life, and it is because of, not in spite of, our misfortune that we grow. Our character is not fully tested until things are not going our way. As I suggested earlier, those who have the courage to succeed in spite of adversity often become an inspiration to us all.

There is a story of the person who goes up to the top of the mountain to attain enlightenment and self-actualization. After a period of time, the person feels complete and is ready to reenter the world to do good and be a way-shower for others. While walking off the mountain, bright and alive in a white flowing robe, an ox cart comes by and splashes mud on the enlightened person's robe. The moment of awareness has arrived. How this person deals with the issue of the world splashing mud, not caring about whom the person is or the person's state of enlightenment, is truly the demonstration of change of consciousness.

Whenever something comes up that you believe might prevent you from accomplishing your goals or dreams, ask yourself, "What can I do to turn this 'negative' into a 'positive'?" "How can I make this work for me rather than against me?"

By learning how to transform obstacles into advantages and attacking challenges head on, you will not only continue to move forward; you will gain the inner strength to deal with anything life brings your way.

Realize that misfortune is a bridge, not a barricade, to greater achievements. It is an opening of doors, not the closing of them. When adversity strikes, don't let it stop you. Promise yourself in advance that you will transform that negative into a positive.

AUTOBIOGRAPHY IN FIVE SHORT CHAPTERS

Here is a wonderful short story written by Portia Nelson that captures a lot of what we have been discussing. As you read through it, see if you can identify where you are in your life.

Chapter I

I walk down the street.
There is a deep hole in the sidewalk.
I fall in.
I am lost … I am helpless.
It takes forever to find a way out.

Chapter II

I walk down the same street.
There is a deep hole in the sidewalk.
I pretend I don't see it.
I fall in again.
I can't believe I am in the same place.
But, it isn't my fault.
It still takes a long time to get out.

Chapter III

I walk down the same street.
There is a deep hole in the sidewalk.
I see it is there.
I still fall in … it's a habit.
My eyes are open.
I know where I am.
It is my fault.
I get out immediately.

Chapter IV

I walk down the same street.
There is a deep hole in the sidewalk.
I walk around it.

Chapter V

I walk down another street.

CHANGE CURVE

"That's me," you say. "I am stuck in Chapter II or III. Why can't I get out? Why do I keep doing the same thing over and over again? Is this my comfort zone?" you ask.

Yes.

"Am I on automatic pilot?" you ponder.

Yes.

"Is there something else that is keeping me here?" you ask hesitantly.

Yes.

There is something called the change curve. It is a wonderful little concept that my brother and his wife, Diamond and River Jameson, founders of the Total Integration Institute, uncovered. It goes something like this.

Here I am cruising down life's road and I hear this soft, sensitive, intuitive voice say to me, "Excuse me, but what you are doing is not going to give you the results you want. You might want to do something different."

This is called "point easy." The gentle voice is heard, but I ignore it because, you know, I want to do what I'm doing, and besides, I'm not hurting anyone. So, I say, "Be quiet, little voice."

Time passes. I continue doing what I'm doing, and I start to feel a little uncomfortable. I'm not in pain, and I'm not really hurting anyone, at least not in any obvious way. I'm at "point dissonance." My little voice is speaking a little louder, but you know, I still like what I'm doing. I'm still enjoying it on some level, and as I said, I'm not in pain. So I say, "Leave me alone, little voice."

Time continues to pass, and I continue with the same pattern of behavior when, all of a sudden, I move into "point pain." "Ouch! I feel pain." I am aware of it. "I hurt. Wow, how did this happen?" I ask.

You would think we would change at this point; however, we rarely do because we have just moved into something called the "survival domain." We as humans really like this. We are, in fact, addicted to it on many levels. If you watch any movie or any newscast, read any novel, or play or watch any sports, you will be thrown into the survival domain. It's that primal fight-or-flight thing. It makes us feel alive. Our adrenaline is pumping, our heart is awake, and our eyes are wide open. "Oh boy! We are feeling!" Because we are now feeling, we keep doing what we've been doing. This is where most of us fall into the victim position. "Why is this happening to me?" If we changed our actions, the pain would disappear, but then we would not be feeling and we would not feel as alive. So we keep doing what we were doing.

Time moves on and—wham. We are at "point crisis." At point crisis, our little voice is yelling at us, saying, "Stop what you are doing! It's not working! Stop now! We are really in trouble!" It is at this point that we often do something different. However, if we have been raised in any type of a dysfunctional family, we just move into our comfort zone. "Ah, this is familiar. I know how to deal with this. I have been here before."

GRAPH OF CHANGE CURVE

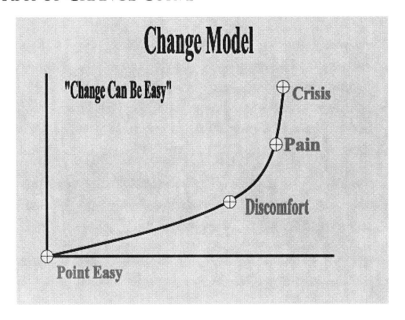

PAYOFFS

Unfortunately, a lot of us are comfortable when we are in crisis. It makes us feel alive, and we as a society seem to be addicted to the adrenaline rush. You say, "It just doesn't make sense that I would choose to stay in a painful situation. What motivates me to do this type of irrational behavior?"

To explain this process of seemingly irrational behavior, let's further explore what motivates us. A friend once told me that if we could figure out what motivates people, we could get them to do just about anything. Madison Avenue advertising campaigns seem to have figured this out. So what is it that motivates us? Or to put it another way, "How can I get you/myself to do the things I want and not do the things I don't want?" We will explore an effective method of creating change within ourselves or others a little later, but for now let's just look at what motivates us.

On a real basic level, it will always come down to the fact that we move either toward pleasure or away from pain. That is it … plain and simple, nothing special about that. We all know that right? So what's the big deal?

The challenge is determining what is painful and what is pleasurable. What is painful to you might be pleasurable to someone else. Or what is pleasurable to you might be painful to someone else. It is really all very subjective.

There are, however, five primary concepts, subcategories of the pain/pleasure principle, that motivate us. They are all important to us; however, we all have a primary and a secondary motivation concept. The five basic concepts are **self-preservation, romance, power, fame, and money.**

Self-preservation is summed up as, "If I don't do it, whatever it is, I will die." That is a pretty big motivation point. In truth, as I've explained earlier, there are only a few things we truly need: air, food, water, shelter, and love. Most of the things we associate with self-preservation are symbols of survival rather than actual things required for survival. However, the mind and body do not distinguish the difference, so getting or not getting these things becomes a matter of life and death in our minds, and we will do just about anything to get them or to avoid them. We are talking real primal stuff here. I am looking outside of myself for a way to feel safe.

Romance is not the traditional romance of falling in love; it is more of a universal helping of others or improving or making the world a better place. "If I do this or don't do this, the world will be a better place for my family, my city, my country, my offspring, and future generations." I am looking outside of myself for fulfillment.

Power is "I have power over you. I am the 'top dog.' You are less than me. I am in control. You do what I want you to do because I know what is best and I am the boss. I like being in control. I like people doing it my way. I am powerful. I am the center of the universe, and I know how it is to be done."

Fame sounds like, "I'm here. Do you see me? You know who I am. When I walk into the room, I want you to notice me and I want you to know who I am. I need to have a lot of attention to validate my existence. I need lots of friends and public notoriety." I am looking outside of myself for approval as a way of building confidence and esteem.

Money is motivating to those who look outside of themselves as a way of feeling complete and feel that money is the primary way to accomplish this. "The more I have, the more successful I am."

To continue to look at what motivates us, I have listed various subcategories of the five basic motivators. They are as follows:

1. Acceptance
2. Approval
3. Praise
4. Love
5. Companionship
6. Greed
7. Punishment
8. Fulfillment
9. Feelings of safety and security

10. Desire to avoid risk

11. Peace

12. Sense of connectedness with a higher power

13. Feeling of righteousness and morality

14. Good nutrition

15. Exercise

16. Proper weight management

17. Healthy sexual expression

18. Feeling of accomplishment

19. Recognition from others

20. Inner awareness of a job well done

21. Being part of a group

22. Feeling you are a contributor

23. Feeling you are a leader

Sometimes, one payoff prevails because it is the path of least resistance. Not all payoffs are obvious. They are always logical, however, even when they seem illogical. In order to understand what motivates your behavior, you can ask yourself, "What is my illogical logic here?"

As I suggested earlier, it always comes back to the primary motivational point of self-preservation: "If I don't do this, I will die."

CHAPTER 5

Patterns To Be Aware Of

ADDICTIVE PATTERNS

One of the most challenging behaviors or patterns to change is an addictive pattern. It is sometimes difficult to understand what motivates us to repeatedly engage in an activity that causes us pain. We know it doesn't serve us. We know it hurts us and others. We know it would benefit us to stop, but we do it anyway.

"Where is the payoff here? It's killing me, yet I keep doing it. I must be crazy."

Possibly. In some of the twelve-step programs, they describe "insanity" as doing the same thing over and over again, expecting different results. In some spiritual organizations, they define "karma" as the inability to stop doing what you are doing even though you know it is causing you pain and suffering. We break or end our insanity or our karma through wisdom. Wisdom comes from the experience of working through our issues consciously.

Let's explore some aspects of the personality and how it is formed to gain some understanding of the addictive pattern process.

Our personality comes from our exterior senses: sight, hearing, smell, taste, and touch.

Our senses can be corrupted by becoming habituated or addicted to certain behaviors or stimuli. This process of habituation is a primal survival technique that is genetically coded so that we do not have to do original learning all the time.

I am in the jungle, and I look at this berry. I recognize it. I ate it last week. It was sweet. I liked it. I felt good after eating it. I didn't get a bellyache or anything. I'll eat it again. There is another berry. It's the same type of berry. Good. I'll eat it again. Oh, another berry. I like these berries. And now I have habituated myself into eating these berries. I have an addiction. I love these berries. Every time I see them, I have to eat them. Unfortunately, I have now found a large patch of berries and I eat all day long. Now I have a bellyache. I feel sick.

Once the senses are addicted or habituated, our personality will want to repeat the experience because it likes it, because it feels good. We are then tempted to repeat the behavior over and over again even if it causes us pain.

A couple of days later, I'm feeling better and I see that berry again. It looks good to me. Is it? What should I do? Should I eat it? I feel confused.

Every time temptation comes in, we split ourselves and our energy. One part says, "I want to do it now!" Another part says, "No, I'm not sure I should do it now."

If we give into our temptations, we are in a roundabout way saying, "I love myself." The eating of the berry was good for me. It felt good. I nourished myself by eating the berry. When I ate the berry, I was good to myself.

Before I explore ways of breaking additive patterns, I want to explain the concept of regular and irregular reward systems and how they affect the way we change our behaviors.

A regular reward system is one that is predictable. I have a lever, and every time I push the lever I get a reward. The reward is pleasurable.

Remember, we move toward pleasure, so we push the lever and we get a reward. It is very predictable. It always works. Every time I push the lever, I get a reward. Wonderful.

An irregular reward system is just that—irregular. In other words, sometimes I push the lever and I get a reward, and other times I push the lever and nothing happens. Nothing happening is painful. As I suggested earlier, we want to avoid pain so we would normally move away from this, but we are not totally sure what will happen when we push the lever. We liked the reward we got when we pushed the lever, so we push the lever again in hopes of getting the reward. If we get the reward again, we are very intrigued and an addiction is being formed. In some ways this is very exciting. We are in the "survival domain" aspect of the change curve I described earlier. We feel alive. The feeling of aliveness is a secondary reward. We often create all kinds of wonderful rituals or superstitions in the irregular reward system. I might put my tongue on the right side of my mouth, push the lever, and get a reward. Wow! I push the lever again with my tongue on the right side of my mouth, and I get a reward again. "This works," I tell myself. From this point forward, I always make sure my tongue is on the right side of my mouth before I push the lever, and it works enough times that this secondary behavior is now attached to the lever pushing and the reward. I now have a dual addiction. These dual addictions or rituals can become very embedded and complicated aspects of our personality. At some point, we find ourselves doing strange things that are now just a part of who we think we are, and we have no conscious idea of where they came from or how they serve us. They are just there.

Now let's say we want to change this behavior of pushing the lever. Under the regular reward system, all we have to do is stop getting the reward, and in a very short period of time, we will stop the behavior. Not receiving the reward is experienced as a painful experience, so we move away from it. We realize the lever is broken, and we move on to another behavior through which we can receive a reward. We seek another pleasurable experience.

If we want to change the behavior of pushing the lever when it has been learned under the irregular reward system, we have a totally different response. We push the lever, and we get no reward. We push it again, no reward. Let's see, maybe I forgot to put my tongue on the right side of my mouth. I put my tongue where it belongs and push the lever, no reward. Hmm. Maybe it's not the right side, maybe it's the left side. I put my tongue on the left side and push the lever, and still I get no reward. Maybe it is on the roof of my mouth. We will continue pushing the lever until we fall over totally exhausted, thinking maybe it will happen with the next push. It worked in the past.

We are chasing the reward, the pleasure, the "high," or the love of the past. We are locked into an addictive pattern and there doesn't seem to be a way out. We are now behaving in a way that looks crazy because we are now hurting ourselves and those around us and we cannot stop. People who care about us tell us what we are doing isn't working, but we are incapable of stopping. We know that pushing this lever works for us. We just know it from the core of our being. And, yet, everyone wants us to change.

As I suggested earlier, the first step to change is awareness.

OK, I am aware this lever no longer gives me the reward I used to get, but I do get some pleasure in pushing it. It is familiar, and that is comforting. So how do I break this addiction or habituated response?

In order to break the habituated response of the senses, we need to move beyond the personality. We need to move into what I call the High Self. The High Self is a neutral character who asks, "If I choose to do this, how will it affect me and how will it affect others around me?"

By asking and answering these questions, we can bypass the addictive personality and begin to make a responsible choice.

By asking and answering these questions, we can also begin to bring in compassion, loving, and caring for ourselves rather than anger and disgust.

When we repeat an addictive behavior pattern that we are in the process of correcting and react with anger and disgust, our energy drops and we disempower ourselves. We often go to fear, which once again calls the addiction forward. Remember that the addictive pattern gives us comfort by being familiar. We often use the addictive pattern as a way to avoid what we are doing, feeling, or seeing. The addictive pattern puts us into a bubble where we are not aware of what is going on. When we are in the bubble, we only think about fulfilling our addiction. The pattern of beating up on ourselves locks us into a pattern of numbing ourselves with an addiction that falsely nurtures us. The punishment we have given ourselves to create change is not effective. Thus, the addictive behavior is repeated and reinforced again and again, and the addictive loop continues with no success in sight.

This is where the five steps to change come into play. Hopefully, you are beginning to see how they are effective in creating change, even when dealing with an addictive pattern.

Our temptations, or our negative addictive patterns, can be used as a tool to strengthen ourselves. They can be used as signals or signs that say, "Where did the 'need' to do this originate?" "How will this serve me?" "What made me start this in the first place?" "Is there another way for me to get what I want rather than doing what I have done in the past?" "What is my intention?" "What other methods could I try to fulfill my intention?" By asking these types of questions, we can begin to take the power away from the addicted senses and create positive conscious change.

After asking and answering these questions, we can bring compassion and forgiveness in by saying to ourselves, "I am sorry for what I did. I was not aware of all of the consequences involved when I began doing this. I forgive myself for my actions and for any judgments I might be holding against myself and others."

I will explore the forgiveness process and how it works in Chapter 5. For now, know it is a way we can release any judgments we might be holding against ourselves for selling out to our exterior senses. If we truly had known better, we would have done better.

It is important to note that not all addictions are bad. As I suggested earlier, the addiction pattern is an aspect of primal survival. Once we are aware that we as humans are addictive creatures, we can use that information for our upliftment, advancement, and growth. All we have to do is get addicted to those things that serve us. Become addicted to healing yourself. Become addicted to forgiving yourself and having compassion for yourself. Become addicted to having joyful, loving people around who support you and encourage you to grow. Become addicted to blessing the people you see, the food you eat, and the people you touch. Become addicted to things that give health, things that set you free and that are for your highest good.

When temptation shows up again or when your addictive pattern knocks on your door, which it will, know this is an opportunity to challenge your addicted senses and to empower your High Self. The process of temptation is called the law of reversibility.

In this discussion of addiction, I would be remiss if I did not talk about the many twelve-step programs that are available today. The first twelve-step program that came into being is AA, or Alcoholics Anonymous. Many other related programs have sprung from this original program. For many, these programs have been a major blessing and a springboard for recovery and freedom. Even though some people have trouble with some of the concepts presented in the programs (mainly a strong direction to total abstinence and a belief in a Higher Power), I have personally witnessed many people achieve and maintain recovery through the twelve steps the various programs teach. Some addictions can be life-threatening, and we often need support as we go through our process. It is nice to know that we are not alone in our process and others have walked before us. It is not necessary to reinvent the wheel. One thing that has always touched me in the programs is the statement "Focus on the similarities, not the differences." We are all individuals, with our own very personal issues, and we are all here on Planet Earth struggling to do our best with the information we have been given. In this we all share similar obstacles in our process to freedom and recovery.

If you want support in your recovery process, you can call your local telephone operator or access the Internet and get the telephone number for AA. From there you will be able to access all of the other programs.

I often say, "The advantage to being clean and sober is that we get to feel." With feelings we can make accurate decisions about our life; we can discern what is effective and what is not.

LAW OF REVERSIBILITY

The law of reversibility is a wonderful law to be aware of. It comes into play any time we make a change in our life. It could be a positive or a negative change. It doesn't matter. Being aware of it and how it works helps us maintain our course of action.

The law of reversibility runs a particular time line. You can almost set your watch to it because of its predictability. The time line is this: three days, seven days, three weeks, three months, six months, one year, three years, and six years.

This is how it works. Let's say I have an addictive pattern of smoking and I want to quit. I have thought about it for a long time, and now I am ready. I do all my preparations, and today is the day. It is going to be hard. I am going to want to smoke all day, but if I have prepared myself, I will make it. Whew! That was tough. But I did it. Day two will also be hard, but I have one day down and I am feeling strong so I get through day two. Day three shows up and all hell breaks loose. I am weak, and the desire to smoke is in my face all day long. Everyone is smoking around me. It smells good. Terrible things happen. I feel spacey, angry, confused, sad, depressed, and abused. Life is not fair. Those two words are in my head all day long. "Screw it! Who cares?" I am challenged again and again. If I get through day three, all of this negative stuff will lighten up. It will not go away, but it will not be as bad. I am now on a roll until day seven, one week from when I quit smoking. "Ugh! It's all here again. I can't take this! Why me? Screw it! I thought life was going to be easier if I quit. It's not. This is hell. It will always be this way. I want a cigarette!" If I get through day seven, it will again lighten up. Week three comes. Here it is again. I am in the same process as before, and it might even be worse. If I get through week three, it will again lighten up. It won't go away completely, but it is much easier. Three months from the time I quit, I feel a freight train has crashed into my life. The process continues until, after six years of being a nonsmoker, I can pretty much know I am home free. I must remain conscious, of course; however, the addictive pattern is behind me for the most part. This does not mean I can indulge in a cigarette here and there. If I do, I will be pulled back into the pattern. It just means I am free from the pattern that was controlling me, that was hurting me.

From my point of view, I think Spirit, or life, has a weird sense of humor. It comes along on this time line and asks the question, "Are you sure? Are you sure you deserve better? Are you sure you are done with that? Don't you want to try it again? Are you sure?" That is the question presented by the law of reversibility.

As I suggested, this same question of "Are you sure?" shows up when we add or create positive addictive patterns as well. Let's say I want to start exercising daily. First day: "Yes! This feels great!" Second day: "I'm a little sore." Third day: "I'm really tired today. I've been good. I don't want to do that. It doesn't really do anything. I don't want to be a fanatic. I'll never have that type of body; it's not in my genes. Besides, I need to do something else today. It's more important than hurting myself with those stupid exercises." The law of reversibility is on me.

Being aware of the law of reversibility and being conscious that we are being asked the question "Are you sure?" gives us another key to creating the changes we want in our life.

CONTINUOUSLY, CONSCIOUSLY CHOOSING

Three little words—"continuously," "consciously," and "choosing"—are primary keys to creating what we want in our lives. I used to think, "OK, I want to be positive or I want to change that behavior. I'm done with that stuff." I thought from that point forward, life would be simple. I had made my decision and I was on my way. I wasn't prepared for the law of reversibility or any of the other stuff we talked about, and five minutes after I had decided to change my behavior, I heard myself being negative and debating in my mind what I should be doing. Somewhere in the process I realized I had to continuously, consciously choose to hold my course of action. If I let go of my conscious choice, I found I was back where I was before. So I had to once again continuously, consciously choose to get back on course again and again and again and again.

A friend of mine said, "It doesn't matter how many times you fall. All you have to do is get up one more time. That is success." As simple as that may sound, I have always been struck by the profoundness of that statement. If you slip and fall and get back into an old addictive pattern, get back up and once again continuously, consciously choose to hold your direction. In time success will be yours to be enjoyed. When? Time and you will tell. You will know when the jar is clean; there will not be any soapsuds. Along the way, judgment will show up. It is part of the human process, as I explained earlier. Use the five steps to change to help you continuously, consciously choose your course of change. Forgiveness is part of this process.

FORGIVENESS

Forgiveness is a process that I am often not in a rush to get to. It is not that I don't feel it is an important part of the healing or the transformational process. On the contrary, I feel it is probably one of the most important steps. Many people want to get there right now. Then all will be well, and they can move on.

I wish it was all that simple. Here is where the "next to every truth stands a lie" concept comes into play, because in some ways, it is all that simple and in others it is not. If we could truly come to a place of forgiveness of ourselves or others, then the issue would be gone and we could go on. Unfortunately, most people are not able to move on, even when they say, "I forgive." They are only mouthing the words, hoping change will come.

Let's say I have smashed my finger with a hammer. After the swelling goes down, the fingernail turns black. I don't want to be aware of the injury, so I put nail polish on my nail. "There. It looks fine. I don't have to deal with it anymore." Except every time I use my finger, I get a twinge of pain. "Ouch! I thought it was fine. It looks OK." I am in denial. I haven't really dealt with the injury. In some ways, this isn't a great analogy because in time my body will heal and my finger will be fine as long as I don't reinjure it.

Our psyche doesn't seem to work the same way. If I have an emotional injury and I ignore it, it doesn't really go away. It comes back again and again, often in a different form, until I learn how to resolve it in a conscious manner. This resolution often looks like the process of acceptance that we explored earlier. Once I have accepted the situation, I have established an attitude of gratitude by changing my altitude. I can feel resolved, and then the process of forgiveness is genuine and meaningful to me and all those involved.

It is at this point that forgiveness becomes a true process of transformation. It allows us to move to a totally different place—a very sacred place called grace. Grace is one of the most wondrous gifts of the universe. Grace means the experience has been transformed. It no longer exits as an "ouch." The experience has become a "keystone" for your upliftment and growth. A very special feeling of peace and joy is experienced and remains through time. There is a major completion.

Let's assume you have done a lot of the writing, burning/tearing, and holding on, you have gone through the process of acceptance, and you feel ready to complete the situation and want to move into forgiveness and grace. What do you say?

The simple answer is, "I forgive myself or whomever was/is involved for …" That would do it. No more, no less. And, often, that is all that is required. However, I have found there are parts of us that feel incomplete with just that, so I have come up with a series of statements that are complete for most people.

As you read through the statements below, be true to yourself. Add or subtract whatever is true for you. In my mind, this is a very precious process deserving of all the tender awareness you can bring forward in the moment.

There are many ways of going through the process. You can read it out loud to yourself, or you can read it out loud to the person you are forgiving. Be aware of the other person's ability to receive the words. A couple doing this together can create an extremely tender space.

As you read the statements, put your name in the blank space. It might sound a little strange to put your name there. Just remember that there are many parts or aspects of ourselves, and you are addressing the part or aspect of yourself that you held a judgment against.

All that _____ has done to offend me, I forgive. Within and without, I forgive. Everything s/he has done to make me angry, bitter, resentful, or frustrated, I forgive. Things past, things present, things future, I forgive. I forgive everything s/he has done that could possibly need my forgiveness. I forgive positively everything. All things are harmonious between us now and forever. I forgive myself for misunderstanding and for judging _____ and myself. I set us both free.

I forgive _____ for hurting me. I forgive _____ for being ignorant of the issue. I forgive _____ for running some assumptions against me. I forgive _____ for being stuck in his/her rightness. I forgive _____ for forgetting who I am. I forgive _____ for forgetting who s/he is. I forgive _____ for forgetting we both are divine.

I forgive myself for getting involved with_____. I forgive myself for failing to see the "signs." I forgive myself for all the bad things that happened. I fully and freely forgive myself. I release myself from all blame. I release all negative or uncomplimentary thoughts and feelings about myself. I release them, lose them, and let them go. I am forgiven and free from all conditions of the past dealing with _____. I forgive myself for all shortcomings, misunderstandings, and confusion. I forgive myself for all feelings and actions I have ever held against myself and others.

You can go through the forgiveness process as many times as you wish. The more conscious you can be when you read these phrases, the deeper you will experience them.

THE MIRROR CONCEPT

The mirror concept is another tool that can assist us in self-awareness and help us to understand what makes us repeat our abusive patterns. Unless we heal and consciously reprogram our inner relationship, our self-talk, we will often continue to repeat our original abusive pattern. We unconsciously select people who complement how we have been raised. We find people (e.g., bosses, lovers, or friends) who treat us the way we have been trained by our primary caregivers. We find people who teach us, discipline us, or love us the way we were taught, the way we were disciplined, and the way we were loved. If this training process was abusive, then we unconsciously find people who abuse us or who repeat our original abuse pattern.

If the people we have selected to be with do not reflect our original abusive pattern, we distort what they think, feel, say, or do until we can pretend it matches up with our original abusive pattern. If our distortion does not work, we provoke the person until s/he wants to treat us the way we were treated in our original abusive pattern. We eventually train them to fulfill our prophecy, making it a self-fulfilling prophecy. We train them to mirror our inner relationship.

In the most simplistic terms, the mirror concept is this: what I like about you is what I like about me, and what I don't like about you is what I don't like about me. This seems obvious in the moment as you reflect on it. However, you probably will feel it doesn't apply when you are in an argument with someone, when you feel you are "right" and they are "wrong," or when you are judging them or their behavior. It still applies. Of course, it just takes a little more awareness and self-reflection to see it.

When we look outside ourselves, we tend to evaluate the world. We look at our reality through our own set of values. Our evaluations can tell us a lot about ourselves and the people around us. If we are aware of this process, we can then use these evaluations, or perceptions, to learn valuable information about who we are and how we perceive ourselves and others.

Whatever we define as the "truth" about the people and things around us is also the "truth" about ourselves. When we evaluate anything outside ourselves, we are looking into a mirror and it is reflecting back to us information about ourselves.

You may not always like what you see in the mirror. However, if you want to learn about yourself more quickly, looking at yourself in the mirror of people and things can be an extremely valuable tool.

If you look at someone and think, "They are angry, and I don't like it." Could it be you don't like it when you are angry? If you look at someone and think, "They are scared. I wish they'd stop procrastinating and just do it." Could there be something you're scared about, something you wish you would "just do"?

To judge and blame others does us little good. By using the mirror concept, however, we can learn how and where we are judging and blaming ourselves. This is information we can do something about. We can stop judging and blaming ourselves, and we can do whatever is necessary to correct the behavior we are judging. We can use the five steps to change and then move into the acceptance and forgiveness process.

Most people, when they discover they are blaming themselves, begin to judge the fact that they are blaming themselves. They enter into a continuous loop of judgment and abuse. Correcting this abusive loop can often seem challenging. It becomes a process of peeling the layers of the proverbial onion.

Sometimes, in order to understand how to use the mirror concept, we have to shift our focus a bit to see what it is about ourselves that's being reflected by others. For example, you may look at someone smoking and not like it. If you use the mirror concept, you might say, "I don't smoke, so that doesn't apply to me." If you reflect on what you are judging when you look at the smoker, you might see someone doing something that is obviously hurting them. They know it is hurting them, yet they continue with the hurtful behavior. At this point, you could ask yourself, "What is it I don't like about the other person's smoking?" "It's unhealthy," you might say. Then, the question becomes, "What do I do that's not in the best interest of my health?" "Smoking is inconsiderate," you might say. What do you do that is inconsiderate? "Smoking is a bad habit." What is your worst habit? "It's a waste of money." What do you waste money on? "It shows no self-control." Where do you lack self-control? What are you doing that is hurting you, yet you keep doing it? I suspect you will find something in here that can be applied to you. If not, then ask yourself, "What have I done in the past that has hurt me and that I have continued doing anyway?"

We observe other people's actions, and then we place judgments on their actions. If we move from the action we judge and look at the judgment, we usually find a similar judgment we make toward ourselves.

You can extend this idea beyond people to inanimate objects as well. "This car never works when I want it to," you might say. What part of you never works when you want it to? "It always rains at the worst possible time," you might say. What do you do at the worst possible time? "This steak is too tough," you might say. What about you could use a little tenderizing?

How does knowing this about yourself help? First, it gives you a lot of material on which to practice acceptance. Can you accept everything you already know about yourself and also everything you learn about yourself by looking into the mirror of other people's behavior? Your harshest judgments of others are the very ones you must accept about yourself.

Second, the mirror also reflects something you can do something about. You're the only one you can really change and the only one who can really use all of your good advice. Ask the question, "How does the advice I want to give someone else fit me?"

If your advice to so-and-so is to be more careful with his money and you don't think you need that advice because you're already very careful with your money, then what do you need to be more careful about? If your advice to so-and-so is to exercise more and you already exercise a lot, what part of yourself, other than your body, could do with a bit more exercise?

When we use the mirror concept and see all the things within ourselves that need improvement, we might be overwhelmed and say, "Oh, this is too much. I don't want to see all of this. I don't want this much information." Know that we are in a process here on Planet Earth. With each step of awareness comes more information. Remember that this is a classroom, and we are in a continual process of learning. Be gentle with yourself. Change what you can now, know you are in process, and love who you are and who you are becoming.

We can also see that whenever we lash out at another, we are really lashing out at ourselves. In this context, to strike another is as silly as striking the mirror in the bathroom because it's giving you a reflection you don't like.

By using the mirror concept, we can also see what's good about us. All the people and things we find loving, affectionate, caring, devoted, tender, wonderful, compassionate, beautiful, adorable, magnificent, and sacred are devoted, tender, wonderful, compassionate, beautiful, adorable, magnificent, and sacred parts of ourselves. Isn't that nice to know? And yet, for some people, the lighter side of the mirror concept can be harder to accept. "I can see that I'm intolerant when I judge someone else for being intolerant," you may say. "But when I see the awesome beauty of the ocean, what does that have to do with me?" Everything! That awesome ocean is an aspect of you.

By using the mirror concept, we can begin to discover the true source of the projections we send out. We can begin to see that other people are an aspect of ourselves. They become what we project onto them. We see other people as wonderful, and so are we. We project our own wonderfulness upon them. The more you use the mirror concept, the more you will find how effectively you can use it for your own growth and upliftment.

THE INNER MIRROR CONCEPT

There is another aspect to the mirror concept that is even more profound than what we have just explored, and it is this: the relationship I have with you is a mirror of the relationship I have with myself.

If I have a harsh, cruel, critical relationship with you, I am suggesting that I will have a harsh, cruel, critical relationship with myself. If, on the other hand, I have a loving, nurturing, supportive relationship with you, then I will have a loving, nurturing, supportive relationship with myself. If I have a loving, nurturing, and supportive relationship with myself and you attempt to be harsh, cruel, and critical with me, I will not let you in. I will not let you get close. I will move away from you because the relationship I have with myself is too precious to be around harsh, cruel, critical people. I will allow only loving, nurturing, and supportive people to get close.

Part of the process of getting healthy is initially changing our relationship with ourselves. We learn how to correct our behavior in an effective, loving way rather than the old electric–shock-treatment way. As we get better at this, something happens. People start falling away. We no longer need punishing, abusive people in our lives. This is good news and bad news. The good news is that we have more love and support around us. The bad news is that some of the people we have been close to for years are no longer around. This includes friends, brothers, sisters, moms, dads, husbands, and wives. We have changed, and we demand those around us to change. We demand that they treat us differently. Some of these people will be able to join us, and some will not. The ones who are not capable of treating us differently will eventually fall away.

I often say, "We can have a healthy, loving relationship with very dysfunctional people." However, in order to have a healthy, loving relationship with dysfunctional people, we have to put subject and time limits on our relationship. I rarely encourage people to divorce members of their family. It is just too hurtful, and we are often left with a deep feeling of regret. I do, however, recommend putting subject and time limits on your relationships with harsh, cruel, and critical people.

How do you do this? you ask. Let me give you a couple examples. Years ago, I was working with a client whose father had been very harsh and extremely critical when he was younger. He hated his father and never wanted to see him again. After a period of time of writing and burning and working on his own self-talk and self-parenting, he began to understand and have compassion toward his father. His father also, probably because of the aging process, had mellowed and had become more accepting of his son. The father, however, remained very controlling and stood in his position of "rightness." The son discovered that he could establish a deep, loving relationship with his dad if he "subject and time limited" his relationship with him. Through trail and error, he discovered he could talk to his dad on the phone for about five to ten minutes every three to four months. By doing this, his relationship with his father healed and deepened. I want to emphasize that this was not a superficial relationship at all. It was very deep and loving. The son had discovered that if he spent more than this amount of time with his dad, he would want to fix his dad or his dad would attempt to control him. He didn't need to be controlled, and his dad didn't need to be fixed. By shaping the relationship within these boundaries, subject and time limiting, the son was able to have a healthy, loving relationship with his father.

I must warn you about using subject and time limiting to create a healthy, loving relationship with dysfunctional people: it works!

Let me explain. Again, years ago, I was working with a woman whose mother was anything but nurturing. Of course, she deeply desired to receive acceptance and nurturance from her mother. Her mother, however, was really incapable of giving acceptance and nurturance. Every time my client would go to her mom for acceptance and nurturance, she would receive harsh and critical words. She would always be chastised.

As my client went through her healing process, she became stronger and stronger, and she began to love and accept herself. She learned how to nurture herself in all types of situations. She also wanted to heal her relationship with her mom, and, as part of that process, she began to subject and time limit her conversations. In so doing, their relationship began to blossom in time. Initially, I must add, her mother noticed her daughter pulling back and responding differently to her regular attacks. The daughter, however, had learned not to take the bait and would graciously avoid a confrontation. The mother's attacks began to diminish, and in time the daughter began to think, "My mom is different. She understands me now. She has changed." At some point, the daughter felt safe to go to her mom for acceptance and nurturance. She actually asked her mom to accept and nurture her. Wham! Right at that moment, her mother reverted back to her old ways and became harsh and critical. Luckily, the daughter was aware enough to know that she let her mom in too close. She forgot that her mom was not capable of giving acceptance and love in certain situations. The daughter again began to subject and time limit her relationship with her mom, and the relationship returned to a healthy one. The daughter once again learned who her mother was and what she was capable of doing. She moved into a place of acceptance.

I share this story so you can be aware of the process and hopefully not get caught and disappointed.

THE INNER FAMILY

It might be helpful to understand how we develop our inner family or our inner relationship with ourselves in order to understand the inner mirror concept. I am going to attempt to keep this real simple, and I'm not going to use a lot of physiological words to confuse you.

Basically, our moms and dads raised us the best way they knew how. I believe that if they knew better, they would have done better. That being said, for the most part, they did some things we all wish they hadn't, and they didn't do some things we all wish they had. At our birth, I doubt they said, "I'm going to really screw this kid up." At our birth, for the most part, they looked at us and loved us, and they wanted us to be good, healthy, productive adults. In order for us to become good, healthy, productive adults, they trained us the way they were trained.

In the "good old days," there was a belief that there was something bad in the child. The concept of "spare the rod, spoil the child" was prevalent. Therefore, parents needed to beat the "hell" out of the child. If I beat the "hell" out of you, then all that will be left is heaven. Because they loved us so much, they had to beat us, they had to be harsh and critical, they had to correct everything we did wrong, and they had to teach a lesson so we would never, ever forget it. They did all of this because they "loved" us. How wonderful.

We were all good students and wanted to make our parents happy, so we unconsciously incorporated all of their methods inside. If we did something "wrong," we would beat the "hell" out of ourselves so we would learn the lesson. If we could do it to ourselves effectively, we would not receive the beating from the world (i.e., our parents, teachers, etc.). We became socialized. Our parents are now inside of our heads, critically yelling at us, and we no longer need them to yell at us in the real world. We hear their voices as we go to do something. We hear them say, "How many times do I have to tell you not to do that! You are so stupid. You will never make it." Or we hear, "Great job. I knew you could do it. I have faith in you. You are so creative and capable." We know how to self-correct, and we do it the way we have been trained by our loving parents. The inner parents we have in our head match the parents or primary caregivers we had in the world when we were younger.

As time passes, we meet someone we love, and as we get close to them, we see they are doing things that they "should not" be doing. So we, out of our love, parent them the way we parent ourselves, the way our parents parented us. We are harsh, cruel, and critical toward our partners because we love them, like our parents loved us, and we want them to be good, healthy, productive adults as well. The end result, of course, is disastrous and often ends in separation and divorce. I will discuss the process of relationships a little later; right now, I just want you to understand how the inner mirror concept works.

The inner mirror concept is this: the relationship I have with you is a mirror of the relationship I have with myself. The relationship I have with myself is a mirror of the relationship I had with my parents. To repeat, if I have a harsh, cruel, critical relationship with myself, I will have a harsh, cruel, critical relationship with you. This suggests that I had a harsh, cruel, critical relationship with my parents. I love you the way they loved me. I train and discipline you the way they trained and disciplined me. If I want a more loving, nurturing relationship with you, I have to create a loving, nurturing relationship with myself, and I have to change my relationship with myself in a loving, nurturing way.

EXERCISES

Below are a few sentence prompts to help you uncover how you were loved and how you were trained to be a good, healthy, productive person. Take a piece of paper and write down the endings of the sentences. After you have written down as much as you can, look inside and be aware of what you are feeling. Do the writing, tearing/burning, and holding on exercise. Be aware of your self-talk, and play with the five steps to change exercise. If it is appropriate, work with the acceptance and forgiveness process.

I wish my mom/dad had …

I wish my mom/dad hadn't …

My mom/dad never …

My mom/dad always …

My mom/dad punished me when I did/didn't …

My mom/dad punished me by doing/not doing …

AN EXAMPLE

I wish my mom had demonstrated her love to me by letting me play the piano and by holding me, by telling me she loved me, by being nice to me, and by helping me clean up my room.

I wish my mom hadn't yelled at us kids all the time. She was always so critical. Everything had to be so perfect. I wish she had let me play more. I wish she had played with me more. I wish she and my dad hadn't fought so much. I wish my dad had been home to protect me from my mom's moods.

My mom never played with me in my room. She never sang to me. She never was happy with what I did. She never let me be me. She never let me move at my own pace.

My mom always yelled at me in front of my friends. She always shamed me. She always took away my toys and made me cry.

My mom punished me when I didn't do it her way. She punished me when I stood up for what I thought was right. She punished me when I ignored her yelling.

My mom punished me by slapping me. She punished me by taking away my favorite toys. She punished me by yelling at me when she was in my face. She punished me by telling me I was a loser, dumb, lazy, and no good.

CHAPTER 6

Boundaries

*Y*ou are now in the process of loving yourself more, and you are aware that there are people in your life who are abusive. You love these people, and yet you now know the relationships you have been having with them are not healthy for you and you want to clean them up. You want to subject and time limit your relationships, but you don't know how to do it in an effective way. This brings us to boundaries. I will now explain what they are and how to set them in a loving, effective way. Boundaries are one of those things that seem to be systematic. As you start to look at your boundaries and how you have set them in the past, you will begin to see that this is an area rich with many opportunities for growth for you and those in your life.

A boundary is a personal limit that allows us to love others without resentment. It allows us to give and receive from others without compromising our own integrity. A boundary enables our inner child, or basic self, to feel safe and nurtured.

We cannot ignore a boundary without paying a price. If a boundary is violated and the situation is not corrected, it will adversely affect the connection between us and the other person in the relationship.

Setting our boundaries clearly is what allows us to be in charge of our peace. The focus is on our behavior, not on controlling the behavior of others.

When we are out of integrity with ourselves, or we are not honoring ourselves and our needs, we will not set clear boundaries with others because we fear we will hurt them. We fear we will get rejected. Or we fear we will feel foolish, embarrassed, or ashamed of our needs.

By setting a boundary, we create the risk of finding out a truth about ourselves, about others, or about our relationship with others.

The less pain we can tolerate, the shorter our reaction time will be in letting others know when and how our boundaries have been violated. The higher our pain tolerance, the more prone we will be to exploding before setting our boundaries.

If we do not know how to be honest with or take care of ourselves, we will focus on controlling the behavior of others as a way to feel comfortable and safe.

If we are unaware of our needs and do not know how to set boundaries, we will do a lot of things we do not want to do, and we will do them with people we do not like.

Sometimes we discover our boundaries <u>after</u> they have been violated. When this occurs, we often feel angry. We blame others and feel resentful.

At other times, we discover our boundaries are being violated in the moment they are being violated. With this discovery, we might not take action even if we are aware of not liking how we are feeling. Over time and with practice, our ability to take action gradually catches up with our awareness. Life is a learning process, and by continuously, consciously choosing, we will get better at responding honestly and lovingly in the moment.

We can also set our boundaries proactively. This is the ideal. It saves time and prevents chaos, crisis, and pain. It is what we are working toward. At first, we have hindsight. We have an experience, and we learn from it. We consciously make course corrections. Then we develop "now sight." We are aware of who we are and how to express ourselves in an effective manner. Then we develop foresight. We know who we are, and as we look into the future, we know our wants and how to express them so others hear us. For the most part, they honor our requests because we set clear, healthy boundaries.

There are times when we inadvertently violate our boundaries because we do not know what to do. A situation might surprise us, or the situation was imperfect and there just was not a good solution. Perhaps it was a new situation that we had never encountered before and we were experiencing original learning. The most important things for us to remember are to forgive ourselves and to use the situation as a learning opportunity. The better we become at setting our boundaries, the fewer times we find ourselves in awkward situations because we are able to stop a lot of situations before they become painful.

When we discover that our boundaries have been violated, we first discharge our feelings using the writing, tearing/burning, and holding on exercise. Then we implement the five steps for change process. We talk to our inner child or basic self and pinpoint the moment we felt violated. We identify, as much as possible, what made us feel uncomfortable. We also look at what kept us from speaking up and expressing our truth. We look for habitual patterns that keep us from setting our boundaries on a consistent basis. We ask, "What did I make more important than keeping my word with myself?" We then begin to create a different scenario in our mind's eye. We make up different responses we could have given. We concentrate on how and when we could have made an earlier intervention. We role play different responses in our mind, dialogue on paper, or role play with a friend until we feel comfortable with our new response. This process cannot be done in a few minutes. It might take us several weeks to fully explore and develop a new scenario.

Sometimes we will want to take a "time out." It is OK for us to delay setting a boundary if we are not sure what we feel or if we do not know how to set boundaries at the time. If this is the case, we can say, "I'm not sure what I feel about this, but I'll get back to you as soon as I do." Or "I'm not comfortable talking about this right at this moment. I need some time to think before I answer you." Or "Let me think about this first." Or "I will need to get back to you on this."

One way we discover what we want is by asking ourselves, "What do I want to get from this? Am I clear about the results I want from the boundary I am setting? What is my intention?" We want to discover what limits we have that keep us from feeling peaceful. We want to know what things we can do that can help us stay in the loving and out of resentment.

When we are ready to disclose our boundaries, we use "I" statements, not "we" or "you" statements. We stay with our own experiences. We do not argue the merits of our case. Our experience or perception of the situation cannot be argued with. It is our experience. It probably is not the other person's experience, but it is ours and that is what we are attempting to communicate so the other person can understand who we are and what we are asking for. We could say, "My experience is_____." "I am willing to do _____. I am not willing to do _____." "What I don't want from you is _____. What I want from you is _____."

When we talk from our experience, we stay out of power struggles and stay centered in our own power. We do not weaken our position by having our attention diverted into points that can't be proven.

For example, "You're not trying hard enough."

"Yes, I am. You just can't see it."

"No, you're not. I know you could do better."

"I am doing better! You never see it."

"Yes, I do. I know when you are being lazy."

"No, you don't!"

"Yes, I do!"

When setting our boundaries, in order to be effective, we speak from our heart and use kind words.

For example, "In the past I was very good at hiding my feelings; I suspect you were not even aware that you were crossing or violating my boundaries. Now, I want you to know who I am and what makes me feel safe when we are together. I want you to know my process so you can understand me. I want you to understand my logic even if it sounds illogical to you. I want you to know me better so we can stay in a loving place with each other."

It is important to match our words with our actions in order for others to understand and trust us. As we continue to grow and expand in our own awareness of ourselves, we will need to revise, clarify, and update our boundaries. As we become aware of these new boundaries, it is our responsibility to share our revisions and updates with others so they know what we are asking of them. They are not mind readers; therefore, it is our job to express our boundaries as clearly as we can with our current awareness and communications skills.

When we express our boundaries, we must be prepared for a variety of reactions. Someone might respond with anger, they might withdraw their loving, they might attempt to make us wrong, or they might not be willing to work out a solution with us.

The gentlest way for us to set our boundaries is to let others know what we are experiencing. This intervention is useful when we are not clear on what we want to be different. We could say, "I don't know what I want to happen between us, but I do know that I am uncomfortable with what is happening right now."

At times, we do know what is necessary for us to honor ourselves. In this type of situation, we could say in a nonshaming, nonmanipulative, respectful way, "It's not OK with me that _____ is going on. I've thought it through, and I have decided to do _____ from now on." Or "I am not comfortable with _____, and _____ is what I'd like to have happen." "I know that I've done _____ for a long time, but I am changing and have decided not to do that anymore. I would like you to _____."

When we set new boundaries, by definition, we change our relationships with others. Our new behavior and boundaries often threaten or make others feel uncomfortable. Therefore, they frequently demand that we change back to the way we were in the past. However, in order for us to remain true to ourselves, these reactions are no longer sufficient reasons for us to abandon our boundaries. It is important to note that we do not need to make the reactions others have to our new boundaries wrong. It is important to listen and communicate in a clear, loving manner. This is a perfect place to do what is called "active listening." I will explain this process in Chapter 11.

If our boundaries are not honored and we need to take another step to protect them, we can make cause and effect statements that are logical, nonpunitive, and realistically enforceable. We focus on actions that we are prepared to follow through with. We know we are free to do what we want to do, and at the same time we are letting others know what actions we will be taking to stay safe. We have given up our desire to control others. We only focus on what we can do to maintain our peace. During this type of situation we could say, "Your choice to _____ is your choice for _____ to occur." "Your choice to _____ is your choice for me to do _____."

For example, "Your choice to <u>continue yelling at me</u> is your choice for <u>me to leave</u>." "Your choice to <u>continue drinking</u> is your choice for <u>us to</u>

separate." "Your choice to <u>continue criticizing me</u> is your choice for <u>me to take a break from our relationship</u>."

As a last resort, in situations where there is physical abuse or where no one is willing to connect or learn, we can take an action without using words. We can just walk away. This is the most intense level of boundary setting because no resolution is being attempted. It is a declaration that the relationship is over.

There is a progression in setting boundaries. We do not start with walking away or with the ultimatum "Your choice to _____ is your choice for me to do _____." This is where we end up if all else fails. We start by making a simple request of what we want in a gentle, loving way. The intention here in setting healthy boundaries is to create a more loving and honoring relationship. The intention is not to hurt or to create separation. Therefore, be gentle with yourself and with others as you learn to set and express healthy boundaries.

SUMMARY

Before we express our new boundaries with someone, we need to do the following:

(1) Write, tear/burn, and hold on as a way to vent anger, resentment, and blaming feelings.

(2) Write a letter that could be shared with the person.

    (2a) Describe in detail the actual events and behaviors, without interpretation, that disturbed you.

    (2b) Describe the feelings it brought up.

    (2c) Describe how this behavior/incident affected your life.

    (2d) Make a clear statement about what was not OK with you.

        "It is not OK with me that you made disparaging remarks to me about my sexuality." "The way you addressed me in the staff meeting today is not OK."

(2e) Clearly request what you want.

"I would like an acknowledgement from you that this happened." "I want you to talk to me about respect."

(2f) Clearly express what the consequences are if the behavior continues.

"If this happens again, I will leave and return when the circumstances are different."

"Rather than staying silent in the future, you can expect me, in this type of situation, to ask you to hold your comments until we can talk privately."

(3) We can express our boundaries in person, on the phone, in a letter, or in an email. The discerning point is to do it in a way we feel safe. If we choose to share our boundaries in person or on the phone, it is important to make an appointment at a time and place that is agreeable to all parties concerned and in an environment where the conversation will not be disturbed.

Sharing our boundaries on this level can be very scary and totally unpredictable, so it is important to prepare for anything to happen. We could come to an agreement and become closer, or the other person could deny or minimize the issue. S/he could attack us with put-downs or explosions, and this could sever our relationship. The end result of sharing our boundaries is an honest relationship based on reality, not illusion or deceit. Thus, the end result is integrity, freedom, love, peace, and joy.

CHECKLIST OF BOUNDARIES IN RELATIONSHIPS

Below is a checklist of boundaries in relationships that has been passed around in many twelve-step programs. I do not know who created it or when it was created, so I cannot acknowledge the person or persons responsible for it. It is, however, a very good list of unhealthy and healthy boundaries. The first time you read the list, you might feel like you are being overloaded with information. I admit, there is a lot here, and it can seem simplistic. However, the information is actually very profound and powerful. So after you read through the list, go back and read just one or two statements at a time and let the subtlety of the statements settle in. Ask yourself how the statements relate to you in your primary and secondary relationships. Ask yourself what changes are required for you to have healthy boundaries in all of your relationships.

Unhealthy
- You are unclear about your preferences
- You don't notice unhappiness since enduring is your concern
- You alter your behavior, plans, or opinions to fit the current moods or circumstance of another (live reactively)
- You do more and more for less and less
- You take as truth the most recent opinion you heard

- You live hopefully while wishing and waiting
- You are satisfied if you are coping and surviving
- You have hobbies because you have no attention span for self-directed activities
- You make exceptions for a person for things you would not tolerate in anyone else/ accept alibis

Healthy
- You have clear preferences and act upon them
- You recognize when you are happy/unhappy
- You acknowledge moods and circumstances around you while remaining centered (live actively)
- You do more when that gets positive results
- You trust your own intuition while being open to others' opinions

- You live optimistically while co-working on change
- You are satisfied when you are thriving
- You have excited interest in self-enhancing hobbies and projects
- You have a personal standard, albeit flexible, that applies to everyone and ask for accountability

- You are manipulated by flattery and you lose objectivity

- You try to create intimacy with a narcissist

- You are so strongly affected by another that obsession results

- You will forsake every personal limit to get sex or the promise of it

- You see your partner causing your excitement

- You feel hurt and victimized but not angry

- You act out of compliance and compromise

- You do favors that you inwardly resist (can't say no)

- You disregard intuition in favor of wishes

- You allow your partner to abuse your children or friends

- You mostly feel afraid and confused

- You are enmeshed in a drama that is beyond your control

- You are living a life that is not yours, and this seems unalterable

- You appreciate feedback and can distinguish it from attempts to manipulate

- You relate to partners with whom mutual love is possible

- You are strongly affected by your partner's behavior and take it as information

- You integrate sex so you can enjoy it but never at the cost of your integrity

- You see your partner stimulating your excitement

- You let yourself feel angry, say "ouch" and embark upon a program of change

- You act out of agreement and negotiation

- You do favors you choose to do (you can say no)

- You honor intuitions and distinguish them from wishes

- You insist others' boundaries be as safe as yours

- You mostly feel secure and clear

- You are always aware of your choices

- You are living a life that approximates what you always wanted for yourself

- You commit yourself for as long as the other needs you to be committed (no bottom line)
- You believe you have no right to secrets

- You decide how, to what extent, and how long you will be committed
- You protect your privacy naturally and honestly

AN EXERCISE

List three situations in which you have a hard time setting a boundary. What do you feel would happen if you set a boundary in these areas?

List three situations where you want to say no but you haven't. By not saying no in these situations, what are you saying yes to?

List any friends or acquaintances with whom you feel unable to set a healthy boundary by saying no. How does your not setting a healthy boundary diminish the quality of the relationships? What do you feel would happen if you set a healthy boundary?

Note any situations in which you feel pressured to say yes. What is the worst thing that would happen if you postponed your answer until you were clear on what you wanted? What is the best thing that could happen?

CHAPTER 7

Ways to Stay Clear

COMMITMENTS

*K*eeping healthy boundaries with ourselves and with others often requires us to make a commitment to ourselves and to others. But what does it mean when we say, "I am making a commitment to …"?

It's the "C" word. It's the word many people are afraid of saying. It's a word that is often misunderstood. If you look up the word "commit" in the dictionary, you will discover that it means "to make a promise." And then we see the suffix "ment" tagged on the end of the word. What does that mean? Whenever you see that at the end of a word, it means it's an inner process. So the word "commitment" means you are promising yourself something. It can also involve someone else, but the primary promise is to yourself.

It is important to know that whenever we make a commitment to ourselves or to anyone else, we always have permission to renegotiate our commitment. You must know, however, that not everyone is going to be happy that you are renegotiating or changing your commitment, but you do have this right.

There is a major difference between breaking a commitment and renegotiating a commitment. Let me explain. Let's say you make a commitment to be somewhere at 7:00 PM. At 6:59 PM, you could call and say, "I want to renegotiate my commitment with you. I am not going to be able to be there at 7:00 PM." You have not broken your commitment with yourself or with the other person. Granted, the other person could be upset, but you are still in your integrity and are still keeping your word.

If, however, you call at 7:01 PM and say that you will not be able to be there on time, you have broken your commitment. You have not kept your word. This might seem like a fine point to be making, and it is; however, this is how precise our basic self or inner child keeps track of what we do and say.

In order for ourselves or others to trust us, it is important for us to keep our word, to keep our commitment. The way we trust someone is by evaluating whether their actions match their words through time. If their actions do not match their words through time, then we no longer trust them and we no longer feel safe. Therefore, it is important to keep your word or commitment with yourself and with others. If you find you are not able to keep your word or commitment, renegotiate. You might be known as someone who always renegotiates with people, and that might be a good reputation to have. People can trust that you will do what you say or that they will hear from you if it is necessary to renegotiate your commitment. Your word can be trusted.

There is great value in keeping our commitments. As I suggested, it creates trust. If we have been in a habit of not keeping our commitments with ourselves, we no longer trust what we say. For example, let's say you tell yourself, "Today, I am going to clean out my closet." Your basic self or inner child hears this and says, "Yeah. I've heard that before. I think I just want to stay here in bed and sleep a little longer. S/he never does what s/he says. S/he is just full of a lot of hot air. I'm tired." You no longer trust yourself or what you say. You feel like a fool and a failure because you never do what you say you're going to do; therefore, you go through life exhausted and depressed with no desire or belief that you can ever change. You are just who you are—"a lazy, no good fool." Notice your self-talk here. Your self-talk begins to reinforce your belief of who you are, and a self-fulfilling prophecy is set in motion and reinforced by your lack of doing, your lack of keeping your commitment with yourself.

"What do I do?" you ask. Use the five steps to change. In the alternative step, one thing you could do is raise the value of your word. Right now your word means very little to you or to your inner child or basic self. If you raise the value of your word, you will increase the likelihood that you will keep your word. Let's say you make that commitment to clean out your closet, you share your commitment with me, and you want me to help you keep your word. Up until now, you have been unable to do what you say you want to do, and you want to change this pattern. My first question to you would be, "Who do you love a lot?" You tell me your grandmother is someone very special in your life and that you love her dearly. I say, "OK, I am going to use your grandmother to help you keep your word. In fact, she is making a commitment to help you keep your word." I know people often don't keep their word, so I have this wonderful contraption to guarantee that your grandmother will help you keep your word. Let me describe my contraption. It has two tall beams going up about fifteen feet in the air, and there is this sharp, heavy blade up there on the top. Your grandmother is beneath the blade with her hands and head locked so that she cannot move. I am standing next to the contraption, holding onto a rope that is connected to that sharp, heavy blade. I am nervous, sweating and shaking a bit, because you just made a commitment with me. By the way, the basket there on the ground under your grandmother's head is there just in case you don't keep your word.

If this were literally the case, would you clean out your closet today? I am sure your answer would be an emphatic yes. In fact, you probably would tell your grandmother, "Hold on, I'm cleaning out my closet right now, and I'm taking pictures so he will believe me. I don't trust this guy. I'm getting you out of this thing as soon as possible. I'll be right back."

All I did was raise the value of your word. I made your word become involved with a life-or-death situation. The truth is that every time you don't do what you say you are going to do, you cut off your own head. You lower your self-esteem and your belief in yourself. You no longer trust yourself.

It is important to keep our commitments with ourselves and others. If we know we are not going to be able to keep our commitments, it is life or death to our self-esteem. Then we renegotiate.

INCOMPLETES

Earlier, I suggested that we feel exhausted when we don't keep our word. You ask, "How does that work?"

We have this very special part of us that I call the basic self or the inner child, which keeps track of everything we say and do. Its primary job is to keep us alive, and it will do whatever it thinks necessary to accomplish this task. Sometimes it's very logical, and sometimes its methods seem very illogical. This process of keeping track of everything is an aspect of its job. It takes its job very seriously. Remember, its job is to keep us alive. It believes we have only so much energy, so it attempts to regulate our energy flow. Let's revisit the closet example (before we brought in grandmother, by the way). You make that commitment to clean out your closet, and your basic self says, "Hmm, that's a pretty big job. I'll put this amount of energy aside for that task." You then commit to reading this book. You basic self says, "Oh, that's a really big task. That makes me feel uncomfortable, and I am always being asked to do or think differently. I'll put this much energy aside for that." Then you decide to commit to calling your mom on her birthday, and you want to get her a gift. Basic self says, "Oh, this will be fun. I get to go shopping, and I love talking to Mom. I'll set aside this much energy." Or if you have a challenging relationship with your mom, your basic self could say, "Ugh! I don't want to do that. I don't know. Just thinking about it takes a lot of energy. I'll set aside this much energy to process the thought."

Get the idea? This inner process goes on all the time. So if you have a lot of incompletes in your life, your basic self has set aside all this energy for all these tasks and you feel exhausted. All of your energy has been assigned, and you don't want to do anything. How do you get your energy back you ask? You get your energy back by completing your incompletes. When you clean out that closet—wham—you get all that energy back. You finish the book—wham—you get more energy. When you buy your mom a present and call her, you get more energy again. And on it goes.

"That's too much. I can't do all of that! I don't have enough time." You are probably right. So let me help you out a little. Remember when I mentioned that we can always renegotiate our commitments? This is where it can help us get current in our lives, reclaim our energy, and develop trust in our basic self.

First, I would ask you make an incomplete list of your incompletes. It will be incomplete because I doubt you will be able to consciously remember everything you have committed to. Once you have your list, read though it and either choose a date by which you can reasonably complete each item or renegotiate with yourself. There are many definitions for the word "complete." It means different things to different people at different times. It is actually a very subjective word. You have permission to define it however you choose. Make sure your definition supports you in your upliftment, advancement, and growth.

I would encourage you not to define completion in a way that hurts or limits you. To be more specific, let's say I have ten books on my nightstand that I say I am going to read. My fifth-grade teacher told me that reading a book meant I was to read each word, and if I didn't understand the word I was reading, then I was to look it up in the dictionary. After I read the book from cover to cover, I was supposed to tell someone what I read and what I learned. This was great advice, by the way; however, I am no longer in the fifth grade. Some of these books I started but don't like, some are poorly written, and some—I don't even know how they got there. So I am going to redefine completion. At this point, completion will be looking at the book, maybe skipping through a few pages, reading a sentence here and there, closing the book, and declaring the reading of the book complete. I move it off my nightstand onto the bookcase, out the door to a library, or into the recycle bin. I have now reclaimed my energy and am free to move on with my life, unencumbered by those ten books weighing on me every night before I go to sleep.

AN EXAMPLE OF AN INCOMPLETE LIST OF INCOMPLETES

List	Action/Decision
Call John about garage	Do by April 10th
Write Uncle Pete	Renegotiate and call by April 20th
Ten books on night stand	Scan and declare complete
Buy new pot for kitchen plant	Give plant away by April 9th
Wash and polish car	Wash car by April 15th; renegotiate on polishing
Clean out closet	Do today to get grandmother free
Clean out trunk	Do when washing car by April 15th
Balance checkbook	Renegotiate and hire Sally to help monthly
Write resume	Renegotiate and call Tom to help
Call Mom and Dad	Do by April 8th
Take magazines to hospital	Do by April 19th

RESENTMENTS

Understanding resentments and how they work in our lives is an important key to joy-filled living. People often carry resentments for years. They have no idea how to get beyond them, except maybe to seek revenge, and that, of course, is not an effective way to resolve them. Resentments are emotions that work closely with boundaries and commitments.

When we look at the word "resentment," we again see that little "ment" tagged on to the end. Therefore, we know resentment is primarily an inner process. If we continue to break down the word "resent," we see two more parts. The first part of the word is "re." This means to do something over and over again. The second part of the word is "sent." This means we are sending a message to someone over and over again. When we put it all together, we discover that resentment means we are *sending a message to ourselves over and over again.*

Interesting, huh? So, on one level, the fastest way to get out of resentment is to deliver the message to the person you are holding the resentment against. Tell the person what you want or what you don't want. This, you now know, is called setting a boundary. It seems pretty simple on one level, yet on another level, you also now know that in order to set healthy boundaries, you have to know what your boundaries are and how to set them in a healthy way. Setting and maintaining healthy boundaries is an ongoing process of discovery and recovery.

There is another level to the resentment process that can be even more profound. If you change your point of view, you can see that resentment is *a biofeedback mechanism telling you that you have given too much.*

Let me explain. Here I am giving to you out of my overflow. I have more than I need, and I just give to you freely. I don't have any expectations. What you do with what I am giving to you is fine with me. I don't have any attachments. It is yours to use however you choose to use it. When I give from my overflow, I have no resentments and I have no expectations.

I continue to give to you out of my overflow, and at some point in time, I am becoming exhausted. Now I am giving to you out of my essence. Now what I am giving to you is precious stuff. Even though I don't have any more to give, I continue to give to you for a variety of reasons. Now, I do expect you to use this my way, and I expect you to really appreciate it. You don't, of course. You just use it like you always have, and you don't seem to appreciate it any more than usual. Now I resent you. You're not doing it the way I think you "should." I feel you are taking me for granted. I feel you are taking advantage of me. I feel victimized. I am angry, and I resent you. I could deliver the message to you. I could say, "I want you to use this stuff the 'right' way, my way, and I want you to really appreciate that I am giving it to you even though I am on empty." This is a reasonable request; however, there is yet another more powerful and effective action I could take.

If I recognize that resentment just means that I am giving too much, then all I have to do is back off a little and give back to myself. All I have to do is fill myself up until I once again have an overflow. When I am full, I can once again give out of my overflow. I am no longer in resentment.

When I back off, I don't need to end the relationship; I just need to back off a little. Walking around the block might be all that is required for me to replenish myself. There are lots of ways to fill ourselves up. I will outline some of the ways later, but for right now, I just want you to understand and explore the concept of resentment. The next time you feel resentment, notice how you are feeling. I am suggesting you will have overcommitted—you will be giving too much. I am suggesting you have placed some expectations on your giving. Some examples could sound like these: "I always call you. You never call me." "I am the one who always has to decide what we are going to do. I don't want that responsibility anymore." "I am the one who always pays for dinner. You seem to expect me to always pick up the bill. Yes, I do have more money than you, but I am tired of being the one to reach in my pocket." "You never take out the trash or wash the dishes. You expect me to always pick up your clothes. I want some help around the house." "I am the one who always gives our children a bath. You just sit there expecting me to do everything. I know you worked all day. I did too. I am tired just like you. I want some help from you."

In these examples, you can hear how the person feels victimized, how they have done too much, and how their expectations are not being met. You can also hear how the person seems to feel like they have a job to do or a specific role to play.

This brings me to the concept of tradition. The word "tradition" means "betrayer of the present." It means what worked yesterday should work today. It means that yesterday I was able to do all these things for you, and therefore I "should" do them today. It means I "should" *always* do these things. It is what we have established as tradition. Many people slip into resentment because they are honoring a tradition. They are maintaining a pattern that no longer works. They are not being true to themselves; they are being true to a tradition. I am not suggesting all traditions are bad. I am suggesting, however, that we look at what we have established as tradition and see if it is still appropriate and still giving us the results we want. If we are going to remain true to ourselves, be honest with others, and not just do what we have done traditionally in the relationship, then we must be willing to question our actions and change our behavior.

GIVING AND RECEIVING

The concept of giving and receiving seems pretty simple and obvious on the surface. However, it can be an area of deep hurt and misunderstanding. I would like to explore giving and receiving on an energetic level so you can see the various dynamics of giving and receiving and know how to give and receive in a healthy manner. As I stated in the last chapter, if you give too much, you will feel resentment. Knowing this helps to discern when giving is appropriate, and it gives a marker or a biofeedback mechanism that tells us when giving is too much or inappropriate.

The other side of the process of giving is receiving. You might ask, "How do I receive in a healthy way? I don't like getting things from others because then I feel obligated. I would just as soon do it myself, thank you."

This is one approach, so let's look at it closer. Let's say you want to give me a gift as a way of saying thank you for something. You give this gift to me because you care and you like to give. Humans just like giving to one another. It is one of those precious things we do. So you want to give me this gift. It can be a big or a small gift, or it can just be a compliment. When you give me the gift, I give it back to you, and I say, "Thank you, but I don't deserve that." At this point you feel hurt, maybe a little angry, and rejected. I didn't want your gift. Isn't that strange? I was polite. I said, "Thank you." I did a little self-depreciation by saying, "I don't deserve that." And you felt hurt because I rejected your gift. It is important to note that every time you say, "No, thank you" to someone giving you something, they feel an aspect of the hurt feelings or anger you felt. As a side note, remember that hurting our feelings is a method we use to get others to do what we want through guilt. You wanted me to accept your gift. I didn't do what you wanted, and you hurt your feelings so I would feel guilty and take your gift. Or you got angry at me and said, "How dare you not take my gift" so that I would do what you wanted and receive your gift through intimidation.

There is another approach available to us. Let's say you want to give me that gift for whatever reason. As you give it to me, I reach out to receive it and say, "Thank you. I appreciate that." Now you feel happy. I received your gift. I was polite; I said "thank you" and all is well. However, after I received your gift, I set it down and I cut any strings you might have attached to your giving. Once you give it to me, it is mine. I could treasure it forever, sell it, give it away, or put it in the recycle bin. It's mine. At this point, I owe you nothing. My job was to receive it. My receiving it completed the act. You might come to me and say, "Would you wash my car?" and I could say, "I'd love to. I love washing cars." Or I could say, "No, I don't like washing cars, and I don't really want to wash your car." You might respond,

"But I gave you that gift." I state, "Yes, you did. Thank you for that, and receiving your gift and washing your car are two separate issues." My job was to receive your gift. I can give it back to you if I want; however, I am not obligated.

This might sound cold and contrary to what some of us have been taught, so check it out. Enlist a friend and ask them to role play giving and receiving. First, ask them to refuse your gift in a nice way. Then, from your heart, give them a gift. They say, "No, thank you." How did that feel? Do it again, only this time they receive your gift and they say, "Thank you." How did that feel? This role play will reveal the value of receiving.

Many people want more abundance in their lives, but they don't know how to receive. In order to be abundant, you have to receive. Years ago, I saw a popular singer completing a tour. It was going to be her last concert for some time. Everyone was aware of this, and this concert was extra special and all her fans were there as a way of saying thank you and goodbye for now. Many had brought flowers and had worked their way to the edge of the stage with their flowers in their hands. All night the singer would go to the edge of the stage and gather flowers and then place them on the stage in a nice arrangement. It was wonderful. There she was, demonstrating receiving and abundance. She didn't need anyone to buy her flowers. She had more money than she could spend, and yet, there she was gathering flowers all night long. Her fans, with glowing smiles, were saying, "She took my flowers!" No one cared what she did with all of those flowers after the concert. She probably gave them to the stage crew or some convalescent home. That was her business; it wasn't ours. Her job was to receive, and she did it in such a beautiful way. I suspect her ability to receive assisted in her becoming so abundant.

EXPECTATIONS

Expectations can result in messy emotions that usually create negative results. If you don't do what I expect you to do, I will be angry, hurt, resentful, disappointed, or pissed off. Basically, if you don't fulfill my expectations, I will not be happy. Negative emotions seem to be connected to our expectations. When I saw this years ago, not wanting to experience so many negative emotions, I began to ask myself every time I had a negative emotion, "What was my expectation here? What was I demanding of you? What result was I attached to? What rule had you broken?" I quickly discovered that you didn't do what I wanted you to do. Knowing I couldn't control you, I decided I just wouldn't have any expectations. Unfortunately, that didn't work. So I came up with an expectation that worked for me. I expect that you as a human being will do what you do.

There are two levels to this expectation. First, humans seem to have a wide variety of ways for doing things. Everyone seems to think that his or her way is the "right" way and expect that others will do something in that wide range of doing. What will you do? I'm not sure; however, it will be exciting and interesting to see what you will actually do. I will watch and see. Oh boy, more fun. There are no hurt feelings here with this approach, just a sense of excitement.

The second level to the expectation that "you as a human being will do what you do" is that what you have done in the past, you will probably do in the future. Humans repeat their behavior, and I expect you will be a human and will probably do today what you did yesterday. Will you? I don't really know. I will watch and see. Again, I am in a state of excitement. I am not running your past on you. However, you probably will do what you have done, and yet humans also are known to change. It is possible you could do something dramatically different. It is another one of those precious things about our species. We are capable of spontaneously changing our minds, our values, and our lives. How exciting. What a wonderful thing. I expect you will fulfill my expectation. I expect you as a human being will do what you do. Now that you are fulfilling my expectations, I have no reason to be upset on any level. Joy is present. What a nice way to walk through life.

I would like to share a story that highlights this point.

A mom sends her child to the store to get five items. The child feels important, and he proudly accepts the responsibility and trots off to the store to get the five items. When the child returns home, he presents three items to his mom. She looks at the delivered goods and says, "What's wrong with you? Are you stupid? I told you to get five items, and you only brought me three. What am I going to do with you? Here are three more items. Go back to the store and bring back these five items." The child again accepts the responsibility with a sense of humbleness, and off to the store he goes. The child returns with three items again. The mother, totally exasperated, says, "You are a loser. I am so tired of you not doing what you are told. You are so dumb. You can't even remember five items. I am sick of you. Here are three more items. Get to the store, and don't forget anything this time!" Of course, the humiliated child returns with three items.

Guess what? Mom is not learning. Her child can remember only three items. The child is not capable of remembering five. Mom's expectations are not appropriate. Her demands and reprimands are creating a child with low self-esteem and negative self-talk. If Mom were being watchful, she could see what the child was capable of doing and have expectations that the child will do what he can do. Then the child would fulfill her expectations, and she would be at peace and reward the child for doing a good job. The child's self-esteem would rise, and in time he would be able to remember four items and then maybe five items.

By changing our expectations to match what "is" not only affects our inner emotional state but also our relationships with others. People will want to be around us more because they receive from us the four things we are all starved for: love, approval, appreciation, and attention. When we demand that others fulfill our expectations, they often fail. Then we get to dump our judgments and disappointments on them, and they walk away feeling beat up and probably wondering if it is worth their time and energy to have a relationship with us at all.

FILLING UP YOUR CUP

How can we fill up our cup when we are running on empty? Most of us have been trained to go outside of ourselves for fulfillment. We are told through the mass media that we will be happy if we drive this car, if we have this type of partner, if we make this amount of money, if we live in this neighborhood, if we get this degree, if we do this, or if we do that.

All of these things have value; however, they don't really fill us up. In fact, once we have them, we often are left with a strange, empty feeling inside and the thought, "Is that all there is?" Having goals and a purpose is important, and having goals and a purpose keeps us from feeling depressed and worthless. The fulfillment of these goals, however, doesn't seem to fill us up.

There are six basic things we can do to fill up and reconnect to our heart or loving. They are being in nature, listening to music, playing with animals, being with babies, touching our physical heart, and going inside to quietly be with ourselves. Experiment and discover what works for you. Remember that we are changing, so what works today might not work tomorrow. Be willing to explore and be flexible as you go through time.

The type of nature you like to be in or the type of music you enjoy is very personal. Discover who you are. There is not a right or wrong way of doing this. You will know what works for you because you will feel a peace come over you as you rediscover your center.

BEING WITH YOUR SELF

I want to explore how we can go inside and quietly be with ourselves in a little more detail. Some people call this process of going inside meditation. I hesitate to use the word "meditation" because is comes with much misunderstanding and many rules and regulations of rights and wrongs. It also has a religious or a spiritual connotation and thus for some a negative connection, so I am going to call this process a way of "being with your self." What I will share is a basic technique that can work for anyone, no matter what their belief system.

The first thing to do is to sit or lie down in a relaxed manner. If you lie down, you have a higher chance of falling asleep, so if you want to be awake and alert during this process, it is best to sit up. How you sit is your business. Just be comfortable. You can put both feet on the floor, or you can tuck them under you. Do what feels comfortable. Relax your arms and let your hands rest in your lap or on your thighs. The main idea here is to be comfortable, relaxed, and open. You can do this anywhere—in Central Park, on a bus, in a train, on a plane, in your bedroom, or next to the ocean. Some people like it quiet; some people like it noisy. For many people, the fewer distractions there are in the immediate environment, the easier it is to go inside and quietly be with themselves. Discover what works best for you.

Now that you are comfortable, take a few deep breaths through your nose and exhale through your mouth. Breathe in as deeply as possible. Breathing deeply is uncomfortable for a lot of people, so be gentle with yourself. As you breathe in, focus on the air coming in through your nose. It will feel cool and fresh. As you exhale, it will feel warm. Continue breathing deeply, attempting to make each succeeding breath deeper than the last. After breathing in this manner for a minute or two, just relax and be with your body. Notice what you are feeling in your shoulders, your heart area, your stomach, the base of the spine, your hip area, your knees, and your feet. Just be aware and notice any tightness, heat, or tingling. You need do nothing with this awareness. Just be aware.

Consciously attempting to clear your mind of all thoughts rarely works. The mind's job is to think, and if you try to force it to be quiet, you will be entering into a losing battle. Therefore, it helps to give your mind something to focus on. Saying the words "in" and "out" as you breathe can help to clear your mind of random thoughts. You can use a variety of words here. You could say "peace" and "joy," or you could say, "(Your name), I am loving you, I am loving you, (Your name)." Find the words that work for you.

As you are sitting, breathing, and focusing your mind on your words, your mind may start racing around thinking about this and that. You can just watch your thinking process, or you can write down your thoughts. It is wise to have a pad and a pen close by to write down your thoughts. You might think, "Oh, I need to get some apples." Gently open your eyes and write down "apples." Close your eyes and focus on your breathing and your words. In a few seconds, you might think, "I want to call Mary." Open your eyes and write down "Call Mary." Close your eyes again and focus on your breathing and your words. After a bit you think, "Wash dishes." Open your eyes and write down "Wash dishes." Close your eyes and focus on your breathing and your words, and then you might think, "Get some apples." Tell yourself, "I already wrote it down." Focus on your breathing and your words. This is the process. After you have been doing this process for a while, there will be less and less note taking, and it will be easier for you to hold your focus on your breathing and your words longer and longer.

How long do you need to sit and be with your self? Start with five minutes. Use a timer, and when it dings, get up and do your day. Do five minutes each day for about two weeks or so. There will be a pull for you to sit longer. When five minutes begins to feel too short of a time, extend your being with your self time to ten minutes. Do the same process as above. Stay at ten minutes for about three months. There is no rush to arrive. It is more important to establish a habitual pattern than to do a marathon session. After about three months of doing ten minutes a day, you might feel a pull to do more. Great! Now do fifteen or twenty minutes a day. This is your time. This is one of the most direct methods of filling up your self. It can become a very special gift to your self.

If you slip out of your routine, just start it again. Do five minutes a day and gradually build up to fifteen or twenty minutes a day. A friend once told me that success is getting up one more time than you fall. It doesn't matter how many times you slip and fall. Just get up one more time.

HOLDING

Besides going inside and being quiet, we also need to be held. We need to be touched. A researcher in the 1970s said we need fifteen hugs a day to maintain health. If this is true, we are all truly starving. And if we are alone, how do we hug ourselves?

I will share three ways we can be held by ourselves and by another human being that can nurture us and help us regain our center when we need affection and attention. All of these techniques are nonsexual. They are just nurturing. However, that does not mean you will be comfortable giving or receiving them because it just might be out of your "comfort zone" to receive this much nurturing. Hopefully, you will be courageous enough to open up and receive the loving and nurturing you deserve.

The first holding technique is you holding yourself. In order to do this, you will need a lightweight blanket, about fifteen to twenty minutes of alone time, and a wall or some sturdy surface to lean up against. Basically, you take the blanket and wrap it around your body while you are standing up. Then you ease yourself down on to the floor in a comfortable sitting position with your thighs up against your chest. Make sure the blanket is tucked in and wrapped all around you. Pull your knees up close to your chest and hold your legs tight against your chest with your arms. This resembles the fetal position. Be careful not to hurt yourself by stressing your back or your knees. This is to be a nurturing exercise. We all have different levels of flexibility, so honor your body. If you want, you can lean up against a wall for support. Once you are in this position, just hold tight, close your eyes, and breathe. If you feel the desire to rock back and forth, then do so in a gentle motion. After a period of time, you will find yourself getting warmer and warmer. You can start to open up the blanket, allowing yourself more movement, and then after fifteen to twenty minutes, you will feel complete. That's it. You have successfully hugged yourself.

Do this as often as you feel depleted, needy, or lonely. If you want to add some positive self-talk during this time, like "(Your name), I am loving you. I am loving you, (Your name)," then that will be an added dimension to the holding process.

The second technique requires two people. One person is to be held; the other person is to hold. This is a very sensitive and precious exercise, and it is to be made clear to all people involved that this is to be a nonsexual experience.

The person who is being held has the hardest job. Their job is just to receive. Just receive. That's it. No giving back. Just receive. That can be a major challenge. Most of us, as I suggested earlier, have been trained to give back in order to balance the act of giving. Your job is to receive. At some other time, it is fine and often nice to hold the person who is giving to you, but this is not to happen during this session. The person who is holding has a very special job of giving. Their job is to just give in the most loving way possible. Your hands are to avoid any sexual parts. You can gently stroke your partner's arms or hair in a loving manner if it feels appropriate. Your primary job is to just hold your partner.

The way you do this is by sitting on the floor with your back up against a wall or some sturdy object so you are comfortable. Your partner then sits between your legs and leans up against your chest so you can wrap your arms around them and hold them. Again, I must stress that this is not in any way to be sexual. It is nurturing. You are holding someone very precious. They are very vulnerable right now. And your job is to protect them and do whatever you can do to make them feel safe so they can receive the loving and nurturing you are giving them.

If it feels appropriate, some gentle rocking can be nice. Listen and sense how your partner is responding to your actions. This is basically a nonverbal action, so keep your verbal communications to a minimum.

Remain in this holding position for fifteen to twenty minutes. Close your eyes and just be. It is fine if you want to use a timer to signal the end, or you can just watch the clock. When the agreed amount of time has been reached, slowly bring the exercise to a close. Remember to be sensitive to the person you have been holding. Let them lead. When it is appropriate, you can share your experiences with each other. It is best to set another time to reverse the positions.

The third holding position is even more delicate and precious. You will want to do this holding technique with someone you feel very close to and safe with. Basically, partner A lies on his/her back and partner B kneels on the floor with his/her knees close to partner A's head so that partner B can lean over and look into partner A's eyes.

From this position, both partners look at each other. When it feels appropriate, partner B slowly leans forward until his/her forehead is touching partner A's forehead. At this point, both partners can close their eyes. Remain in this position for only about five to ten minutes. When it feels time to end the exercise, partner B slowly ends the contact by sitting up. It is important to do this very, very slowly. When your heads are about ten inches or so apart, you can pause and look into each other's eyes again. Then partner B very slowly continues to sit up. It is nice to remain silent for a few minutes, allowing time for both partners to reflect on their own experiences.

When it is appropriate, both partners can sit and face each other and share their thoughts and feelings. This can be a very sacred time, so be gentle and loving with each other.

LET'S LAUGH TOGETHER

It's been said that laughter is good for you. It is true?

Bertrand Babinet, an acupuncturist and a researcher in humanistic psychology, recently did some investigation on laughing. I find the results very profound and exciting. According to Babinet, there are basically four laughing patterns or sounds. They are ho, ho, ho; hay, hay, hay; ha, ha, ha; and he, he, he. Each pattern or sound affects us physically and psychologically in some very specific ways.

The "ho, ho, ho" sound affects the lower part of the body, just below the belly button and down. It strengthens the pelvis, the urogenital functions, the lower back, and the legs. Psychologically, it provides a sense of empowerment. It helps us reclaim our personal power in areas where we usually let our fears run us.

The "hay, hay, hay" sound affects the belly area and the digestive function by strengthening the stomach, spleen, small intestine, liver, gallbladder, pancreas, and the large intestine. Psychologically, it releases resentment, anger, frustration, low self-esteem, lack of self-confidence, attachment, unhealthy dependency issues, the fear of making mistakes, and the sense of feeling victimized.

The "ha, ha, ha" sound affects the rib cage. It strengthens all the body parts in or connected to the rib cage, including the lungs, heart, thymus, thyroid and parathyroid glands, sternum, collarbone, shoulders, thoracic vertebrae, arms, and hands. Psychologically, it releases issues of isolation, separation, depression, and lack of participation in life. It cancels feelings of rejection, abandonment, betrayal, and disappointment. This sound also opens the heart, thus generating courage, generosity, gratitude, and a willingness to be of service.

The "he, he, he" sound affects the head area. It opens the sinuses and releases muscle tension in the jaw, temples, head, neck, and shoulders. It is also a great sacral-cranial adjuster because it sends a resonating wave from the head all the way down the spinal column to the sacrum and the tailbone. It releases all the tension in the face, thus helping us look younger. Psychologically, it brings clarity to our thoughts, cancels wrongs, and brings lightness to our consciousness. It also brings a sense of freedom, joy, and the presence of spirit.

If all this is true, it's time we all laugh, and laugh, and laugh some more. As always, be a scientist and check it out. The worst that could happen is that people would see you laughing and might think life is treating you well. My challenge to you is to use each sound for fifteen to thirty seconds a day for one week and keep track of what you experience.

CHAPTER 8

Depression and Anxiety

*N*ow that we are laughing throughout the day, it is time to explore the two major issues of depression and anxiety. Most people have experienced some form of depression and anxiety or know someone they care about who has struggled with them. What is depression? What is anxiety? And how can we get out of our depression or anxiety?

These are the three questions I hope to answer. However, my answers are not the definitive answers to all the questions. They will just be answers. Hopefully, they will lead you to a better understanding of depression and anxiety and you will discover a way of setting yourself free from these two conditions.

My explanation of depression and anxiety, and the way out of them, may at first appear simplistic, and in some ways it is; however, I would encourage you to once again be a scientist, check it out, and see how it fits for you.

We feel depressed when we are thinking about the past. We feel anxious when we are thinking about the future. The way out of depression and anxiety is to be in the moment. That's it. End of story. It's short, simple, and sweet.

For those of you who are in disbelief or shock, let's look at depression and anxiety a little more closely.

As I stated above, I am suggesting that we feel depressed when we are thinking of the past. When we are thinking of the past and feeling depressed, we are thinking about things that we wish we had done or had not done. We either went too far or not far enough. We fell short of our expectations or the expectations of someone outside of ourselves whom we valued. We keep thinking and thinking and thinking about these things that we did until we get locked into a continuous loop. There seems to be no way out. The more we think about this stuff, the less we move; the less we move, the more we think; and the loop is doubly reinforced because now we are tired, and all we want to do is to go to sleep so we won't have to think about this stuff anymore. Only the loop is locked in now, and we toss and turn or slip into one of those dreams that repeats itself over and over. We are now locked into the loop in our sleep state. Now all we can think about is how we could not sleep last night and our recurring bad dreams. The longer we get locked into this continuous loop, the deeper we sink into depression. It feels like there is no way out.

As I indicated above, one way out of depression is being in the moment. Being in the moment is the point where the past meets the future. It is a point that continually moves forward. It continually changes. It also continually gets smaller and smaller. It is important to note here that staying in the moment all of the time is something that very few people are able to accomplish. It is something to strive toward and to use as a reference point. If you are in the moment, then you can feel your breath flowing in and out of your lungs. You can feel the cool air coming in and the warm air flowing out. You can hear the sounds close by and the sounds far in the distance. If you are really quiet and in the moment, you can even hear your heartbeat and feel the air making contact with your skin and the pressure of your shoes on your toes. You feel how your body is resting on the surface you are sitting on. You can taste the taste in your mouth or sense the lack of taste. You can smell your clothes, the air in your room, the fragrance of flowers in a garden, or the scent of auto exhaust. In the moment, we are able to contact all of our senses and identify what is being seen, heard, felt, smelled, or tasted. Holding a focus on our senses brings us out of the past and into the present.

You might be saying, "Yeah, but how long do I have to do this? I can do it for about five seconds and then I start thinking about all the things I haven't done or all that stuff again. It is too hard to do this."

It is a challenge, I agree. Moving out of depression is not necessarily easy; however, it is simple. Let me add another part to this process of being in the moment that tends to make it easier.

As long as you stay in your chair watching TV or lying in your bed counting the cracks in the wall for the 10,000th time, your energy will be heavy and stay in the continuous loop. Your thoughts become heavy and weigh you down. Your thoughts are depressing you. If you pull yourself into a fetal position, then your energy cycles around even faster. You are truly stuck. What you need to do is move. You must get up and move. It does not matter where or what you do, you just have to move. As you are moving, identify what your senses are picking up. Moving and being with your senses will put you and keep you in the moment. You can go for a walk or wash your dishes or car. Just move. I want you to know that there will be a part of you that will say, "No, I don't want to move. I just want to sit here and be depressed. I don't deserve to be happy. I am no good, and I just can't do anything about it." If these thoughts are coming in, it is a clear indication that you have moved out of the moment and into the past.

There is another side to this equation that I have not discussed yet, and that is anxiety. As I indicated above, we feel anxious when we think about the future. The future is one of those things that never "goes away" and yet never arrives. It just seems to sit there looming over us. What will happen in the future? We don't know. We can make some guesses, but we truly do not know what is going to happen. We can plan and plan and plan, and yet the future remains untouchable and unknowable.

Fear is another word that we could use to describe anxiety. It contains an acronym that holds its definition. The "F" in fear stands for "false," the "E" stands for "expectations," the "A" stands for "appearing," and the "R" stands for "real." So, fear is "false expectations appearing real." The feeling of fear is real; the source of the fear is what is false. The source appears real, however only in rare situations is the source deserving of the emotional reaction of fear. One situation that could be considered appropriate would be when a saber-toothed tiger jumps off a cliff in front of you. Another situation would be when someone is threatening your life. For most of us, these things will never happen.

What most of us do is fantasize about what we think is going to happen in the future and respond to our negative fantasy with fear. We could say that we are choosing to lose in our fantasies. We are creating false expectations that appear real. We are living in the future and not in the moment.

The way out of fear or anxiety is to be in the moment. As with depression, we need to contact our senses and identify exactly what is going on now— not what we think is going on, but what is actually going on. This might sound simple; however, most of us erroneously think what we "think" is correct. Many times it is just our opinion or point of view of what is going on. When we contact our senses and identify what we see, hear, feel, taste, or touch, we move out of our subjective reality and into an objective reality. As with depression, we will have a part of us that will not want to be in the moment. It will want to stay in the created fantasy because it is convinced it is right. If this is the case, know that you are again out of the moment and into the future, pretending or fantasizing about what you think is going on. The endless loop persists when you think you are right and are determined to hold your position of rightness.

Many of us will move from the past to the future. We will be depressed one minute about what we have or have not done in the past and then slip into anxiety over seeing no hope for change in the future. Realizing that tomorrow will be just like today, we become locked into another continuous loop between depression and anxiety. Again, the way out is to be in the moment.

You might be saying, "Yeah, but if I am always in the moment, how can I get anything done?"

If you are truly in the moment, you will no longer be depressed or anxious, and that is movement. And it is only in the moment that we can do anything. It is truly the only place in which we can respond to our environment. It is the position of action and strength.

Now that you have the concept of depression and anxiety, let's see if we can take it to a practical level. You say, "Great, be in the moment. Now what? What do I do now? I don't want to just be in the moment. That is not enough for me."

Great! The question I ask then is, "How can you use your depression or anxiety for your upliftment, advancement, or growth?"

Remember the concept of anger? If we look at depression and anxiety, we see that they are perpetuated by feelings that we did not get what we wanted or that we are afraid that we would not get what we wanted. Hmm. Look familiar? This is a great opportunity to do some writing, tearing or burning, and holding on. We could also use the five steps to change to break our habitual process. Alternatively, we could do "ha, ha, ha" sounds for depression or the "ho, ho, ho" sounds for anxiety. This is another opportunity for us to continuously, consciously choose to transform our life.

CHAPTER 9

Vows

*B*ased on our past experiences, we often make vows or decisions on how we will handle life and all that it brings to us. Often, in the moment, these vows appear true and appropriate. When we make a vow, we usually say, "I will never ..." or "I will always ..." Vows are an aspect of the automatic pilot process we discussed earlier. As time passes, we learn how to deal with these various situations in more uplifting ways, and some of our old vows are no longer appropriate for us. Most of us forget about these vows, and we attempt to go on with our lives with our new approach. However, sometimes it feels like there is some invisible block that just keeps us from fulfilling what we want to do. Upon reflection, we often find some vow we made when we were younger. Our vow is just sitting there as a silent sentry, protecting us from reexperiencing some great emotional pain. Unfortunately, it is also keeping us from experiencing what we want to experience.

You might ask, "How can I clear these old vows? I am not aware of them, yet I feel they are blocking me from getting what I want."

Below is an affirmation that can assist you in clearing limiting vows. As you read the affirmation, put the subject you would like released or cleared in the blank space. You can release vows about romantic relationships, money, sex, marriage, parents, work, abundance, playing, stress, health, food, time, procrastination, or any other subject that comes to mind.

The affirmation for clearing vows is, "For the highest good of all concerned, I rescind any and all negative or limiting vows that have blocked or restricted me concerning _____. I declare these vows null and void. I release these vows, the causes for the vows, the reasons for the causes, and all the effects of these vows."

For some people, saying the above affirmation once is all that is required. Others need to say it many times until all the layers of the vow have been cleared and released.

CHAPTER 10

Healing of Memories

The process of healing of memories is probably one of the most powerful keys I could share with you. It is also probably the most challenging to understand and to do. I also feel there are appropriate and inappropriate times to use it. If you use it too soon, it could be akin to painting fingernail polish over a smashed fingernail and then displaying it as healed. However, after the finger has been healed, putting nail polish on can be an expression of nurturing and loving. It isn't done to hide anything; it is done to enhance something.

"When is it appropriate?" you ask.

Earlier, I talked about cleaning dirty jars. I suggested a jar would be clean when only clear water came out. I suggested a feeling of neutrality would be present. This is the point at which the healing of memory process is the most appropriate and the most powerful. Only you can decide when it is appropriate to do this process.

Before I share how to do the healing of memory process, we need to explore a couple of concepts. The first concept is that the mind and body do not know the difference between imagined or real reality.

Let's play for a little bit. Take a deep breath and just relax. I want you to have an experience of what we are talking about. Take another deep breath and let go of any of that tension that you might be holding in your shoulders. Just relax. Now imagine that you are standing at the ground floor of a forty-seven–story building. As you are standing there, look up, way up. See those clouds up there at the top of the building? It looks a little windy way up there. OK, relax and take another deep breath, and imagine yourself walking through the fancy glass doors of this tall building and walking over to the elevators. Go ahead and look around and notice whether you see anyone else. Now reach out and touch the button that is marked "Up." When the elevator doors open, step inside. Notice the smell. It is a new building, so notice how the new, fresh carpet smells. Locate the control panel inside the elevator, and push the button marked "T," which stands for the top floor. The elevator doors close with a mechanical sound, and the elevator begins its journey up forty-seven floors. Notice that your stomach is dropping down a little and your heart is beginning to pound. Your ears are popping as the elevator continues to make its climb. When it arrives at the top floor, you feel a bit of a lurch as the elevator comes to a brisk stop. The doors open, and as you step out, notice that you are in a long hallway. As you are walking down the hallway, you can see a sign at the far end that says "STAIRS TO ROOF." As you're walking toward that door, notice what is going on. Feel your pulse increasing. It is a green door, and it opens with a creaking sound. As you begin your ascent up the flight of stairs, the door slams shut behind you. Once you are at the top of the stairs, there is another door with another sign stating in bold red letters, "DANGER—HIGH WINDS." Go ahead and open the door, and as you do, feel the wind pushing the door back against your shoulder. Push harder and step onto the roof. As you start to walk on the roof, notice that you are wearing flat shoes that are without any tread and that there seems to be a lot of loose gravel under your soles. It feels slippery, and it is hard to keep your balance as you walk, or crawl, to the edge of the building. Once you are at the edge of the roof, just place your toes over and look down, all the way down to the street that lays forty-seven stories below. The people appear to be tiny little ants, and the cars are the size of matchboxes. Take a deep breath as a gust of wind blows against your back and up your neck, pushing you even closer to the edge. Slowly, being very careful, turn and walk back to the door you just came out of. Open it, quickly descend the stairs to the hallway, get inside the elevator, and push the button marked "GF" for the ground floor. Down you go, and the door opens, allowing you to walk back out onto the street. Take another deep breath as you look up once again and allow yourself to relax. Take another breath. It is OK; you are safe.

Notice what you have been feeling. Your heart is probably still pounding fast. Notice whether you have an anxious feeling in your stomach. You are safe and have been safe throughout this entire process, and yet you have been responding to words on a page and pictures you have been creating in your mind. The mind and body do not know the difference between imagined reality and real reality.

We have the ability to visualize what we want, and there is a part of us that begins to believe what we visualize as a reality. We then begin to act as if it is a reality until it becomes a reality. "Now wait a minute," you say. "I am not going to lie to myself about stuff." My point of view is that we already do lie to ourselves all the time. The paper you are reading looks solid, yet after a physics class we learn that there is more space in the piece of paper than there is mass. Yet we lie to ourselves and pretend that it is solid. There are many lies that we hold inside ourselves as truths that limit us and hold us back from having the success in life that we say we want. These lies can be called limiting beliefs. I will talk more about limiting beliefs later. For now, I would like you to just entertain and play with the idea that the mind and body do not know the difference between imagined reality and real reality.

The second concept I want to explore is memory. Memory is what we think happened to us. Is it what happened? It certainly is what we think happened. However, other people experiencing the same event will have a different memory. So which is the truth? Truth is a point of view. As strange as it seems, truth is very subjective. We all view it differently. For the most part, we see it in a similar manner and agree on it, but we all have our very own truth of what happened. A parent's memory of an event is often very different from a child's memory of the same event. Which is the truth?

They both are. So what we remember as the truth is our truth. Remember, the mind and body don't know the difference. It is our truth, and that is what we must deal with.

Memory is something we remember or what we re-create. It is a picture of what we thought happened, with an emotion wrapped around it, and it has a decision, often recorded in our unconscious as a vow, about ourselves, others, and life. This decision is made so that we can go through life without ever getting hurt again.

For example, let's say my mother and father got divorced when I was three years old, and they left me with my grandparents so I would be safe while they got their lives straightened out. Because of this experience, as a three-year-old, I would feel a great sense of abandonment. I could decide that people I love leave me after three years or so. Never wanting to feel that level of loss again, I decide to only have relationships that last about two years or so. Therefore, I will avoid that huge loss. How ingenious I am. However, now as an adult, I want to have a long-term relationship with someone I love, but for some reason, I just can't get past that two-and-a-half-year mark.

We are multidimensional beings. There are many ways of understanding this. One way is to realize that all of our selves are alive and well inside of us. From the point of conception until now, all ages are here. The one-year-old, the teenager, the twenty-eight-year-old—every age is present inside of us. Those aspects of us have not gone anywhere. For the most part, we are not aware of these different selves, but they are still present. Remember the iceberg concept.

In the example above, it is easy to see that the three-year-old is running the relationship show. And unless I consciously educate and heal the wound as the three-year-old perceived or remembers the wound, the three-year-old will control the adult.

This is where the "healing of memories" process comes into play. Remember, the mind and body do not know the difference between imagined or real reality. A memory is a picture with an emotion wrapped around it. It results from a decision about ourselves, others, and life. The decision maker is usually a younger part of us that did the best it could with the information it had at the time, and now as adults we want to update or change the decision making process. The child's memories and decisions about how to survive limit and block us from fully experiencing our lives. They keep us stuck. These memories do not set us free.

After we have expressed ourselves with the writing, burning or tearing, and holding on process, we can go inside and create a new memory with a new emotion and a new decision about ourselves and about life. You might say, "But you are lying to yourself." And my response is, "Yes, I am." However, as I suggested earlier, it is all subjective; it's all a point of view. We are all lying to ourselves all the time. The difference is that one lie keeps me stuck in the past and the other one sets me free.

What we are essentially doing is reparenting or reeducating our younger selves with the wisdom we have acquired through time.

Enough concepts. Let's just do it so you can have your own experience.

Create a place where you can spend ten or fifteen minutes without being disturbed. Turn off your phone and anything else that might disturb you. When you are comfortable, sitting in a peaceful setting, take five deep breaths, inhaling through the nose and exhaling through the mouth. On the fifth breath, hold and tighten all the muscles in your body. Release your breath and relax. Just be with your body for a minute or two. Repeat this procedure two more times.

Remember when you were a child. The first picture that comes up is where you want to start. Notice what you are wearing, where you are, who is with you, what exactly is going on, and what you are doing and feeling.

Make this as real as possible. If you don't remember exactly what you were wearing or what was in the surrounding environment, make it up.

Allow yourself to be present with the feelings the child experienced at that time. This can be a lonely or scary memory, or it can be a positive memory. At first, I would recommend choosing a situation that is fresh, and I would not start with a major trauma. You are learning a new skill here, so be gentle with yourself. Go slowly. There is no major rush. You are in the process of reparenting your inner parents so they can reparent your inner child.

Using your creative imagination, visualize your adult self, the person you are now, with you as the child in your memory. Freeze any other people who might be in the picture at this time. Approach your child gently and reassure the child that you are not going to hurt or embarrass him/her. You just want to be there to talk with and help the child. Continue to assure your inner child by saying, "I am here to protect you. You don't have to be alone anymore." Allow the child to determine how fast and how far you go. If it is all right with the child, you can give him/her a hug and let him/her know that you love him/her. If the child does not want to be touched, then honor his/her boundaries. The child is the boss here. As strange as it might sound, the child does not necessarily recognize you, and you might be a scary adult to be avoided. It is very important not to rush the child's process.

After you have established communication and trust, ask the child if s/he wants anything from you. Give the child whatever s/he wants. If the child wants ice cream before dinner, then give him/her ice cream. If s/he wants to play outside, then let him/her play outside. Let the child know that you will be there, making sure s/he will be safe.

Ask the child if s/he wants you to change the situation s/he is experiencing. If the child says no, then honor that. If the child says yes, then proceed to change it the way the child wants it to be changed.

Using your creative imagination, take some magic dust out of your pocket and sprinkle it around. Change the situation into one with a loving, supportive outcome. Allow the child to experience what you have created and to express the emotions that are present. This can be challenging, and you might not know what a loving, supportive outcome could be the first time through. This is OK. We are not looking for perfection here. You are learning how to heal a part of you that has been wounded for a long time, and as you master this process, the ways you and your inner child want to change the situation will change. Remember that there are many layers of an onion. Each change is part of the process of healing.

Again, ask the child if s/he wants anything else from you. Honor what the child wants. Continue to do this until you and the child feel complete and resolved for now. You don't have to do it all in one sitting. In fact, it might be best to do just a little at a time.

Before completing the process, ask the child what color of light s/he would like to be surrounded with. Whatever color the child wants, see this colored light surrounding the child and you with lots of love and tenderness for his/her highest good. This is done to create a safe space for the inner child.

If the child will let you, give him/her a hug. Tell him/her that you love and support him/her, and give assurance that s/he will never have to be alone and that you will always be there for him/her.

End by saying goodbye and assuring the child that you will come back again to assist him/her in growing and learning.

It is most effective to do the above process at least once a day for thirty-two days. Using a calendar as a way of keeping track, you can place a star or a heart on each day you connect with your inner child. The thirty-two days help to establish a new pattern deep within you. If you are not able to do it for thirty-two days, don't beat up on yourself. I am just giving you the optimum. You will do what you do. If you only do this once, it will start to create a change within you.

After doing a general healing of memories throughout your childhood for thirty-two days, you can do another thirty-two-day process to heal all your relationships, your experiences with money, or any other major issue in your life that you want to change.

A CALENDAR TO KEEP TRACK OF YOUR PROGRESS

Monday	Tuesday	Wednesday	Thursday	Friday	Saturday	Sunday
♥	♥	♥	♥	♥	♥	♥
♥	♥	♥	♥	♥	♥	♥
♥	♥	♥	♥	♥	♥	♥
♥	♥	♥	♥	♥	♥	♥
♥	♥	♥	♥	♥	♥	♥

AN EXAMPLE

Let's say I had a terrible second-grade teacher. She shamed me in front of my peers. She told me I was lazy and stupid, that I talked too much, and that I was like a monkey and couldn't stay in my seat. From that point on, my educational performance was set and I hated learning. I didn't like school, and I hated sitting in classrooms. All I wanted to do was go outside, play on the playground, and laugh and be silly with my classmates. My grades suffered, and I became an average student who just got by with C's.

As I begin to do my healing work, I remember Ms. Brown and all the times she scolded me. I felt so ashamed and bad. I realized, as I remembered my second-grade experience, how my educational approach had been set. Upon awareness, I find I am angry at her for not seeing me as the creative, curious, energetic child I was. I get out some paper and begin to write about my anger and hurt. I remember other teachers I did battle with, and I write about them as well. I also find I am angry at my mom and dad for not standing up for me and talking to Ms. Brown about who I was. Before her, I loved to read and had a thirst for learning. I write about all the other times my parents didn't protect me or listen to me. After doing this for a while, I find the anger is just a quiet ember inside. I decide it is time to do some healing of memory sessions on my educational experiences.

I get comfortable, close my eyes, and do the breathing exercise as a way to center myself and to quiet my mind. I see myself in Ms. Brown's second-grade class. I have on a striped T-shirt, blue jeans, black high-top sneakers (the kind that came up around the ankles), and white socks. I had a crew cut at the time, which I hated, and I have lots of neat toys in my pockets. I am at my desk. She is talking about something, saying, "Blah, blah, blah," and I reach into my pocket and find my favorite cat-eye marble. I pull it out, look into it, and find myself transported into a world of glass with blue and green colors swirling around. I follow the swirls into another universe of magic and mystery. From far, far away I hear, "Robert? Robert! Robert!!" A hand violently grabs my marble, and I feel Ms. Brown pulling on my T-shirt, dragging me to the front of the room and plopping me down on a stool next to her desk. I feel my brow dripping with sweat as I lower my eyes from my classmates' snickering faces.

I feel my heart beating as the memory flashes in my mind. I breathe deeply, calming myself so I can do the healing of memory exercise.

I freeze everyone in the classroom, including Ms. Brown. I see myself as the adult man I am, and I walk into the classroom and approach that terrified little seven-year-old named Robert. I get down on one knee so I am not scary to him, and I begin to gently, lovingly talk to him. I tell him, "I am here for you. You don't have to be alone anymore. I am not going to let anyone hurt you or embarrass you anymore. I am going to take care of you and protect you because I love you very much." As I look into his eyes, a look of relief begins to show up. I ask him what he wants. He says, "I want to go outside and play. I want to walk in the woods and catch tadpoles in the creek." I smile at him and give him my hand. We walk out together and head for the creek that he told me about. We play and talk. I ask him how school is going and what he thinks about Ms. Brown. He tells me he hates her because she doesn't like him. I listen. He continues to tell me all the things she has taken from him, and now she has taken his favorite cat-eye marble. I continue to listen, letting him know how much I care. When he quiets down, I ask him if he would like to have a better relationship with Ms. Brown. At first he says, "No! She doesn't like me and I'm afraid of her." I assure him we can change things if he wants. After much thought, he agrees to try to change his relationship with her. I tell him he is not bad. I tell him how creative and smart he is and how all we have to do is let Ms. Brown know this in a way she can understand. He is not sure she will ever like him and continues to be frightened. With time, patience, and gentle words, we explore how we can talk to her so she can appreciate and celebrate him. I tell him about this magic dust I often use for this type of situation. After more exploration, he agrees to return to the classroom. I sprinkle the magic dust around, and sure enough, Ms. Brown is different. She sees him and apologizes for not acknowledging his creativity. She returns all the toys she took from him. At this point, he tells me that this is all he wants to do for now. I hear his request and ask him if he would like to come back to this situation again. He says, "Yes. And I would like to change some other things too next time." I acknowledge his courage to revisit this uncomfortable time. He smiles. I ask him what color of light he would like to be surrounded with. He tells me, "Yellow." I see him, myself, Ms. Brown, and all of his classmates surrounded with the beautiful yellow light. I freeze everyone but the two of us, and we sit and talk some more as we get to know each other better.

I allow this scene to fade as I bring myself back to my current waking state. I take a few deep breaths and drink some water to ground myself. I place a mark on my calendar, and my day continues.

I have effectively changed a childhood memory. Has my life changed? At this point, probably not. However, a lot of things have occurred. Remember the concept, "It's not the issue that's the issue; it's how we deal with the issue that's the issue." I have planted a seed inside myself of a new way of looking at my educational experience. I have more to work on; however, the belief that I was a bad boy is being challenged. I am beginning to have new self-talk; I am learning how to listen and how to talk to myself in an effective manner. I am learning how to approach life from a caring point of view rather than from a scolding, fear-based point of view. If I continued to work on my second-grade experience, I would, after a few days, advance to another time, perhaps my ninth-grade algebra experience, my twelfth-grade final exam experience, and my college experiences until all my educational experiences had been explored and healed. I could then look at my relationship experiences as well, going through each relationship I had from my first girlfriend in first grade to the present time.

After I explore how to have a healthy, vibrant, intimate, and committed relationship, I will give an example of how to do a relationship healing-of-memory process.

CHAPTER 11

Relationships

*N*ow that you have worked with healing your relationship with yourself and your inner child, it is time to explore how to have a healthy relationship with someone outside of yourself. There are a couple of things to be aware of here. You are the one you are looking for. You are your soul mate. Every one outside of you is a mirror of the relationship you have with yourself. You are the one you will be with until "death do us part." Anytime we look outside of ourselves for fulfillment, we set ourselves up for disappointment. At least one of four things will happen with anyone you ever get involved with: they will leave, you will leave, they will die, or you will die. In each of these situations, hurt and loss are part of the deal. There is no way you can have a relationship without experiencing anger or hurt. Remember that anger and hurt are tools we use to get ourselves or others to do what we want. Our partners will not always do what we want them to do; therefore, anger and hurt are aspects of all of our relationships.

If all of this is true, and I would encourage you to challenge and explore all of the statements above, why would we want to have a relationship at all, much less an intimate, committed relationship?

My answer is simple: we want a relationship because the love and the growth we share makes it all worth it.

I look at relationships like classrooms. We enter into a classroom to learn something. When we learn what we are to learn, we get to graduate. A classroom can last from one night to a lifetime. Each has its own value.

From my point of view, if you learn one thing about yourself, relationships, or life, then the classroom, the relationship, has been a success. Many people believe only those relationships that last a lifetime are considered to be successful, but I can't buy into that mind-set.

We are living in different times. If we go back 150 years or so, men and women generally died in their mid-thirties or forties. Today, most people will be living well into their seventies and many into their eighties and nineties. Time is different and change is upon us, and along with that, the dynamics of relationships have also changed. Men loving women, women loving men, men loving men, and women loving women are becoming more accepted. The structure of the family has also changed. In the past, women and children were seen as chattel or property to be used. Today, the demand of equality in all aspects of a relationship is seen as healthy. We no longer have nine children to help plant and cultivate the crops; one or two children are perceived as the norm. We demand more from our partners, and our partners demand more from us.

We are all growing. What was considered healthy or normal in the 1950s is now considered to be dysfunctional, codependent, or enmeshed. Sorting it all out requires us all to explore and discover what works and what doesn't. This exploration is both exciting and terrifying. We are in a time when we have changed most of the rules. I will attempt to wade through all of the changes and present a look that will hopefully give you some helpful keys and a methodology to navigate through your relationships.

As a place to begin, I would like to share with you some points that Terri Gorski, an author and therapist, presented in a workshop. He suggests that there are basically three types of relationships: compulsive, apathetic, and healthy.

In a compulsive relationship, both partners say, "I need you!" Both partners crave intensity; however, they often don't have common interests or values. They are looking for an intense, mind-blowing high. In an apathetic relationship, both partners are looking to avoid pain. They live together very comfortably, with little involvement and no expectations. They do not bond. They primarily fulfill their own needs. In a healthy relationship, the partners say, "I want you." They share closeness with mutual respect, excitement, passion, safety, and comfort. They experience ups and downs as part of life's gifts. They are committed to each other and to themselves, and they have shared values, interests, and goals.

In a compulsive relationship, both partners expect magic. They have exaggerated ideal images with high romance and passion as the cornerstone. They expect their partners to act contrary to their nature. They are willing to give up themselves for their partners, and their partners are supposed to do the same. People in an apathetic relationship have no expectations or demands at all. "If I do not expect anything from you, then you cannot hurt me or disappoint me." They are both free to do what they want. In a healthy relationship, the partners have rational expectations that are realistic. They know each other and accept each other before they make a commitment. They also know that they do not always get what they want, even though they communicate their wants clearly.

In a compulsive relationship, both partners expect instant, mood-altering gratification on demand to fix all of their problems now. "You have to satisfy me on my terms and at my speed." They do not really love each other; they love what their partners can do to them and when it stops working, they find another partner. In an apathetic relationship, there are no expectations except the agreement that they will not hurt each other. "You gratify me by making me feel safe and comfortable." In a healthy relationship, both partners expect long-term gratification. They have intense times and quiet times. They make mistakes and their partners make mistakes, and they learn and grow from their mistakes. There is no pattern. They are grateful for the moment and all the surprises it brings. They know they are not responsible for their partners' moods. They love each other for who they are and for what they do.

In a compulsive relationship, both partners disclose everything right now. It is all or nothing. "If you love me, you will take all of my baggage and carry it for me now." In an apathetic relationship, the partners have minimal communication. They do not reveal very much at all. "The less you know about me, the less you can hurt me." Both partners insulate themselves. In a healthy relationship, both partners are honest and maintain their own integrity. Through time, they communicate who they are when it is appropriate. They do not share their deep secrets prematurely.

In a compulsive relationship, one or both have the need for absolute control. They want to manipulate how their partners think, feel, and act. "If I do not control you, then you will hurt me or abandon me." In an apathetic relationship, both partners control each other through abandoning each other. It is passive control. "It is not what I say that counts; it is what I don't say or what I don't do that counts." They control by not talking about their hurts, disappointments, anger, fear, or needs. Neither partner is willing or able to put themselves on the line. They make their partners guess what they want. "When I make you guess what I want, you are usually wrong, which proves to me that I cannot trust you, and therefore I close off even more." In a healthy relationship, both partners share the power. Control over the other is not necessary. Neither partner needs to force or manipulate the other partner into doing what they want them to do. They do not have to prove who is right or wrong or who is better because they feel safe and trust each other. They know their partners would not intentionally hurt them, and they are strong enough to heal if hurt occurs. They do not compete with each other. They support each other's strengths.

In a compulsive relationship, both partners have irrational trust. They trust their partners will change the way we want them to change because "my partner loves me." In an apathetic relationship, the partners have an arrangement to stay at arm's length so there really is no risk of getting hurt. There is no real need for trust. They just coexist and emotionally vegetate together. In a healthy relationship, both partners have rational trust. "I trust you to be what I know you to be. I trust you to be yourself."

In a compulsive relationship, both partners' boundaries merge together. They lose themselves in their partners and expect their partners to do the same. Their partners are supposed to take on their emotional state. "If you don't, then you don't love me." It's a "lose me or lose you" situation. In an apathetic relationship, both partners have rigid boundary agreements that keep them from getting too close. They might be going in the same direction, but they are not together. They can see each other, but they can't really touch each other. They are both afraid to reach out. In a healthy relationship, both partners have flexible boundaries. They have a lot of choices. They can touch, be separate, be alone, be quiet, or be silly. They do not need to change each other. They can be themselves in the relationship. They love their partners for who they are. They have "you," "me," and "us." It is a shared relationship.

In a compulsive relationship, the couple isolates itself from the world. "It's you and me against the world. We're different, and no one understands what we have." They fear their friends will not accept their partners, so they ignore their friends and family. In an apathetic relationship, the couple socializes separately. They do not share their friends. In a healthy relationship, the couple is socially integrated. "I have my friends and you have your friends, and as a couple we share a social network of friends."

In a compulsive relationship, both partners experience repeated cycles of pain and disappointment. They take desperate actions to solve their problems. They will do anything to get pleasure. They want to fix it now. In an apathetic relationship, both partners experience repeated cycles of alienation. All problems produce pain, so they both attempt to avoid the pain by avoiding life. They therefore feel they are powerless, hopeless victims. In a healthy relationship, both partners experience repeated cycles of contentment and satisfaction. They know problems come with life, and they use their "problems" as an opportunity to grow and expand. They are mutually supportive of each other. They work together with concern for each other, as they each stretch to meet the challenges in front of them. A primary affirmation for the relationship is, "Oh boy, more fun!"

All of these descriptions might seem simplistic and polarized, and in many ways they are. In making these simplistic distinctions, however, you can begin to discern where you are in the relationship picture. Which style of relationship do you identify with most? Did you feel uncomfortable or get upset reading certain sections? This might indicate a hot spot for you to explore. The healthy relationship model is not static; it is a goal to strive toward. If you experience an "ouch" in your relationship, you probably are off course and need to do some course correction.

CHART OF BOUNDARIES IN COMPULSIVE, APATHETIC AND HEALTHY RELATIONSHIPS

Compulsive	Apathetic	Healthy
I need you.	I have no expectations.	I want you.
Give me high passion and romance.	Do what you want, just don't hurt me.	I know and accept you.
I expect you will fix me.	I will never bother you.	We learn and grow together.
It's all or nothing.	We have minimal communication.	We share our strengths and weaknesses.
I need to have absolute control.	I let you do whatever you want.	We share and support each other in making decisions.
We have irrational trust.	We coexist and emotionally vegetate.	I trust you to be yourself.

Compulsive	Apathetic	Healthy
Our boundaries merge together.	It's you and me against the world. We ignore our friends and family.	We experience cycles of pain and disappointment.
We have rigid boundaries that keep us from getting too close.	We usually socialize separately. We rarely share friends.	We experience repeated cycles of aloneness.
We have flexible boundaries.	We are socially integrated. We have our own friends, and we share our friends.	We experience repeated cycles of contentment and satisfaction. We grow and expand.

There is an old saying that fits here. If you like the results that you have, then keep doing what you are doing. If you don't like the results that you have, then you have to do something different. What that difference is must be revealed through communication with your partner and often through trail and error. Usually both partners have to change either their attitudes or their actions. It isn't an issue of "fixing" him/her. It is a relationship, and both partners are 100 percent responsible for the relationship working. It is not a 50/50 deal. It is a 100/100 deal.

To clarify how we often get into trouble in a relationship, let's look at some basic relationship principles.

THREE PRINCIPLES TO HELP DEVELOP AND MAINTAIN A HEALTHY RELATIONSHIP

The three basic principles to developing and maintaining a healthy relationship are subtle, profound, and can be somewhat challenging to fulfill.

First, any action that produces bad feelings in you is not good for your relationship with others. This principle ties into the concept of resentment, which we explored in Chapter 7. Remember, if we give out of our overflow, we have no expectations. Our actions are freely given, and we do not expect anything in return. However, if we begin to give out of our essence and start to develop resentment because our partner is not capable of fulfilling our hidden expectations, our act of "kindness" now produces a bad feeling of resentment within us. Unless we resolve the issue of giving too much, our kind acts will eventually destroy the relationship. Another way of saying this is that anything you do for the sake of the relationship that creates a dislike for yourself or the other person will eventually destroy the relationship.

Second, anything that creates good feelings inside of you is good for your relationship with others. I like this one. This means if I do something for you and I enjoy the doing or the giving of the act, then I am supporting the relationship and myself. Therefore, the relationship will grow. This may seem pretty obvious, but sometimes the obvious needs to be stated. Doing things that create joy and loving inside of myself is good for my relationship with you. The point of awareness is to make sure that I am doing my giving out of my overflow while staying free from expectations of getting something back from you. The value of giving love and joy is the feeling of the love and joy in the act of giving.

Third, we get what we focus on, so focus on what you want more of. If I want more love in the relationship, I need to focus on the moments I receive love. If I focus on the moments you are upset, I will get more upsetting moments. If I focus on how often you complain, all I will hear is you complaining. This highlights how many people fall out of love in a long-term relationship. They focus on what they don't like and what they want less of. Magically, the things that bother us increase.

For example, speaking from a man's point of view, let's say I look at a woman and I say to myself, "Wow! She is so beautiful. Look at her hair, her eyes, and her lips. I just love the sound of her voice. She is so wonderful.

I love her!" I am programming my mind to fall in love with her. Like a computer, my mind just receives and uses the information I put in it. I am now in love with her, and we spend more and more time with each other as time passes. Now when I look at her, my self-talk is, "Oh God, can you believe she is doing that again? How stupid. How many times do I have to tell her I hate that? Her hair is disgusting today. And get a load of those shoes. I can't believe I am with someone whose breath smells like that. Ugh!" I am now programming myself to fall out of love with her. In a long-term, healthy, loving relationship I continuously, consciously choose to fall in love with her. In other words, I focus on what I want more of. If I want more joy, I focus on our joy-filled moments, our love-filled moments, and the times we appreciate each other. Remember, we are all starved for love, approval, appreciation, and attention, and if we give our partners these things when they say or do what gives us joy, our partners will do more of the things that give us joy.

SOME POSITIVE THOUGHTS TO CONTINUOUSLY, CONSCIOUSLY CHOOSE

Below is a series of positive thoughts to focus on to help develop and maintain a healthy relationship through time. Holding a positive focus is an ongoing process.

I am proud of him/her.

My family and friends accept and love him/her.

I think s/he is smart and intelligent.

I love his/her hands and feet.

S/he satisfies and appreciates me sexually.

S/he nurtures me.

S/he loves me for my athletic ability.

S/he allows and encourages me to excel.

S/he loves me for who I am on all levels.

There is room for him/her in my life.

S/he loves my body.

I love his/her body.

S/he appreciates my energy.

S/he wants and enjoys being around me.

S/he compliments me.

S/he is someone who I can be with for a long time.

I can be myself around him/her.

S/he is my lover and my best friend.

S/he truly loves and likes me for who I am.

S/he nurtures me emotionally.

S/he thinks I am really terrific when I am just myself.

S/he accepts me for who I am and what I have.

S/he loves me for my intelligence.

I feel safe with him/her.

S/he nurtures me.

S/he is trustworthy.

S/he is light, joyful, and fun, and s/he sees me as being light, joyful, and fun.

S/he appreciates my energy.

S/he appreciates my intelligence.

S/he stimulates and motivates me to do physical activities.

S/he is attracted to me physically.

S/he compliments me on my appearance, my intelligence, and my essence.

S/he gives me space to grow and to be myself.

I can be myself when I am with him/her.

S/he is comfortable with herself/himself.

NINE QUESTIONS TO HELP DEVELOP AND MAINTAIN A HEALTHY RELATIONSHIP

Now that you know the basic principles to help develop and maintain a healthy relationship, how do you know if you are fulfilling or following the principles? The easy answer is that if you are off course or not following the principles, you will feel an "ouch." The ouch might be a big ouch or a small ouch. Below are nine questions that can point you toward a specific area when you feel that ouch, when you are off course, thus allowing yourself to correct your course quickly. Remember, we cannot change anything until we are aware of it. These questions can assist us in looking into specific areas so that we can become aware of where we might be missing the mark.

If you answer yes to any of the questions below, then your actions, in time, will eventually destroy your relationship. The course correction to each of the questions is the opposite of the question. This is easy to point out, but for many of us it can be challenging to take the corrective action. The keys presented earlier in this book give methods to effectively change our behavior. It is important to remember that a relationship is a classroom. It is through being in relationships that we get to learn things about ourselves, and others, on a deeply profound level. Entering into a primary relationship is like climbing down off the mountaintop with our "enlightenment" and then having someone we love splash mud on our white robe. A relationship is where we get to walk our talk. When we feel an ouch, we know the class has begun. As you read though the nine questions, be aware of what you are feeling. Watch for your judgments against yourself and your partner. How can you use the concept of acceptance or the five steps to change here?

1. Am I overly inhibiting myself in this relationship?

2. Am I acting toward the person in ways that would cause me to dislike myself or the other person?

3. Am I ridiculing, criticizing, or blaming the other person?

4. Am I pretending to be somebody that I am not?

5. Am I putting him/her on a pedestal?

6. After I have married the person or am living with him/her, am I putting pressure on him/her to change his/her way of life?

7. Am I allowing the person to mistreat me, believing that these things do not matter if the relationship is good?

8. Am I setting different standards of behavior for my partner and myself?

9. Am I acting differently when I am with him/her than when s/he is not present?

UNREALISTIC BELIEFS ABOUT LOVE AND ROMANCE IN SONGS, ROMANCE NOVELS, AND MOVIES

We all have been lied to. Most of us believed it when we sang our favorite song, "You are the only one! I will die with out you in my life! I can't sleep unless you are in my arms!" We felt it to be true. We sang from our core and cried from our core when we sang, "You left me for another! I will never be the same. I am lost without you!"

Little did we know that by singing along to the radio, we were programming our unconscious to think and feel a certain way. My challenge to you is to consciously listen to ten songs on your favorite radio program or CD and pay attention to what is being said. How are you being programmed? I have a feeling you will be shocked. After you listen to those songs, review the latest romance novel you read. What do you see there? Then watch a couple of soap operas. I know I am walking on very thin ice here, but just take a look. What do you see? Do you see honest, clear communication with integrity? Or do you see deceit, secrets, and lies? If we are wise, we can learn what to do by seeing what doesn't work. Unfortunately, most of us get lost in the story and are being unconsciously programmed to believe that love and romance are something out there that someone is to give to us, or to do to us or for us. Now look at the big movie screen. We see people falling in love, and they seem to stay like that forever. Again, what are the messages we are learning about love? I am not suggesting that you stop listening to music, stop reading romance novels, or stop watching soaps or movies. I just want you to be aware of the programming you are unconsciously receiving.

Below is a list of some of the unrealistic expectations that we have been taught to fulfill in our primary relationships. After you read through the list, I suspect you will have a better understanding of why many people find primary relationships a disappointing and painful experience.

SOME UNREALISTIC BELIEFS

I'm totally and always obsessed with beautiful thoughts about the one
    I love.

The one I love is the perfect person for me.

When you fall in love, it's like two magnets being drawn together, and
    nothing can ever pull them apart.

Being in love is the sweetest feeling in the world.

When you are in love, nothing else matters.

Being in love is feeling completely cozy with someone else.

The person you fall in love with is the most beautiful person in the
    world—perfect, with no flaws.

Love is blind.

Love and romance are the same thing.

When I meet the "right one" and "fall in love," the rest of my life will be perfect.

When you're in love, the rest of the world becomes beautiful.

The one I love is all things to me; s/he fills up my life completely.

The one I love is the half that makes me whole.

When I am away from the one I love, my life is diminished.

If I am not with that person, then I am being rejected and should "pine" and miss him/her all the time.

If I am happy away from him/her, then I don't love him/her that much.

I will do anything to "make it up" to him/her if s/he is hurt or feels bad.

S/he must want to be with me all the time or I'm doing something wrong.

If the one that I love goes away, I am left with a terrible emptiness in my life and only that one person can fill me up and make me feel whole again.

Being in love is wanting to spend every minute of every day with that person, even if you can't.

Being in the presence of the one I love is the most beautiful experience in the world.

Being in love gives my life all the excitement, adventure, variety, and fun I could ever want.

When two people are in love, all they need is each other to be completely fulfilled.

Love is a completely overwhelming feeling of beauty, joy, and adoration toward him/her.

Being in love is like living in a soft-focus movie: everything is sort of hazy and blissful and sugar coated.

When I am in love, *all* my problems will go away!

After you listen to those songs, reread some of those romance novels, and watch your favorite soap opera or the most recent love story, write down what you heard and saw. Use this as an opportunity for awareness. Don't let yourself go into judgment. That creates separation. Judgment is not an effective tool for change. Just be aware. Remember, the first step to change is awareness.

Now that you are aware of how we have been programmed to fail in our primary relations with these unrealistic beliefs, you might ask, "What beliefs can we have that are realistic? What beliefs will help me create a healthy, loving, long-term relationship?"

REALISTIC BELIEFS TO HELP CREATE A HEALTHY, LOVING, LONG-TERM RELATIONSHIP

"So what are some realistic beliefs? You just about destroyed my ability to listen to the radio, and reading my romance novels or watching my favorite soaps will never be the same. Where do I go to learn what is healthy? What is realistic? Can't I have fun in a relationship? Does it always have to be a classroom where I am learning stuff all the time? I have fallen in love, and all the trees did 'whisper Louise.' And I have felt lonely when my partner wasn't next to me, and I felt better when s/he was next to me. I think you are lying to me."

Remember, next to every truth stands a lie. The challenging thing is that "love" does do all of those wonderful things, and yet there is so much more. Going beyond the infatuation stage in a relationship requires us to expand the limited pictures that are presented in the media. It requires a bigger, more expansive look. So let's expand ourselves and see if we can come up with some realistic beliefs about relationships that will take us through time with someone we love.

The list below is not conclusive. It is really only a beginning, and I would encourage you to challenge each item in it. I'd also like to encourage you to add to this list those beliefs that are true for you that I did not include.

SOME REALISTIC BELIEFS

Loving someone means accepting them just as they are.

People who love each other respect each other.

Love is caring about someone.

Love is trusting while understanding that we are all human and mistakes happen.

A loving relationship allows everyone room to grow and develop.

Loving someone means our lives are intertwined and there is room for individual expression.

Loving someone means we give them the dignity of choosing their own path.

People who love each other listen to each other with a desire to understand.

People who love each other support and encourage each other.

People who love each other forgive each other.

People who love each other enjoy each other's company.

Love is an emotion and a feeling, not an absolute reality.

Loving someone does not solve any problems; it may even bring its own problems.

To love someone is a process—a continuing process—not a fact.

When I love someone, I am constantly presented with choices that can either bring me closer or take me further away from the person. It's up to me to make those choices and accept responsibility for the consequences of them.

Life changes; people change; relationships change; love changes.

Love feeds on itself; the more I give, the more I have to give.

I am able to have a loving relationship with someone else to the degree that I have a loving relationship with myself.

Love is like fertilizer; it encourages things to grow.

Love is not confining, smothering, or restrictive.

Love is intimacy.

Love allows me to be vulnerable, so I feel safe enough to let you see me as I really am.

Love is true, good, and honest.

Love wants the best for everything and everyone.

Love is not had at the expense of anyone or anything.

A loving relationship is one of mutual respect and honesty tempered by concern for each other's feelings.

Love and sexual attraction are not the same thing, although it is wonderful when they occur together.

A loving relationship is a bond between people, a bond of shared feelings.

A loving relationship is mutual respect and familiarity with shared experiences.

Love is saying you're sorry when you make a mistake.

LOVE OR INFATUATION

How do you know if what you are feeling is love or infatuation? Are your feelings real and can you trust them? These are the questions most people ask themselves when they first get involved in a relationship. And, to be honest, you really won't know for sure until time has passed. The old saying is that infatuation runs its course in about three months. And in a long-term healthy relationship, you are going to feel some of the feeling of infatuation at the beginning of the relationship. There is a classic Greek story that deals with this notion. The fact that the ancient Greeks had a story dealing with this suggests that it has been a challenging question regarding relationships for centuries. If the story sounds sexist to you, please go beyond that level of seeing and catch the deeper meaning. This issue of discerning between love and infatuation has been challenging to both sexes.

As the story goes, a young man leaves his kingdom to find his bride. As he is leaving his kingdom, he has to cross a large body of water. At the shoreline stands a boat with an old, ugly witch to row him across the water. He of course commissions her to row him to the distant shore. During the crossing, they engage in conversation, and she asks him about his journey. He tells her he is off to find his bride. She asks him if he would like a love potion to help bring her to him. "Yes! Of course!" he replies. As a good witch, she brews up her magic potion right there in the boat, and he drinks it. About this time, they arrive at the distant shore and he departs with confidence and a bounce in his step. In a very short time, he finds the most wonderful woman in the world. He immediately asks her to marry him. She says yes, and they get married. Now it is time to return home, and he finds the boat at the water's edge where he came ashore. The witch is nowhere to be found, so he puts his new wife in the boat and begins rowing across the large body of water. In the middle of the journey across the water, the love potion wears off, and his lovely bride turns into the old, ugly witch. Infatuation had run its course. Illusions and fantasies became reality.

So how do you discern what you are feeling? One primary thing will be time, but as time passes, there are other keys or signs to watch for. Below are some comparison points, which can give you clarity.

Infatuation is instant desire. It is one set of glands calling to another.

Love is friendship that has caught fire. It takes root and grows, one day
    at a time.

Infatuation is marked by a feeling of insecurity. You are excited and eager
    but not genuinely happy. There are nagging doubts, unanswered

questions, and little pieces about your beloved that you would just as soon not examine too closely. It might spoil the dream.

Love is quiet understanding and a mature acceptance of each other's imperfections. It is real. It gives you strength and grows beyond you. You are warmed by his/her presence even when s/he is away. Miles do not separate you. You want him/her nearer. But near or far, you know s/he is yours, and you can wait.

Infatuation says, "We must have each other right away. I don't want to risk losing him/her."

Love says, "Be patient. Don't panic. Plan your future with confidence." You can't lose what is yours.

Infatuation has an element of sexual excitement. It is difficult to be in each other's company unless you are sure it will end in intimacy.

Love is the maturation of friendship. You must be friends as well as lovers.

Infatuation lacks confidence and trust. When s/he is away, you wonder if s/he is cheating. Sometimes you check.

Love means trust. You are calm, secure, and not threatened. S/he feels that trust, and it makes him/her even more trustworthy.

Infatuation might lead you to do things you may regret later.

Love leads you to fulfillment, peace, joy, awareness, learning, and growth.

WHAT WE WANT FROM EACH OTHER

We often hear men say, "Women. Who can figure them out? They are a puzzle to me?" And we hear women say, "Men. I can't figure them out. They are silent, mysterious, and in their cave all the time. They really confuse me."

After hearing this for years, I decided to go around and ask women what they wanted from men and ask men what they wanted from women. To my surprise, the two sexes wanted basically the same things. The differences were interesting and educational.

Below you will find a list of some of the things women and men say they want from each other. As you read through the list, feel free to add or subtract those things that are appropriate to you. You might think of this as a work in progress or as a reference point to what others say they want. If you are in a relationship now, take some time and share this with your partner, discussing what is accurate and what isn't. We don't come with a book of instructions, and most of us are not mind readers, therefore verbal communication is of paramount importance in any relationship and even more so in a primary relationship. If you are not in a relationship at the moment, ask around and see if this list matches what you find. The mystery of the sexes can be resolved through communication.

WHAT SOME WOMEN WANT

A man who: Stimulates her mentally

Makes her laugh and laughs with her

Is a good companion

Is open

Is loving

Likes to share himself with her

Flirts with her

Is warm and affectionate

Has the same sexual appetite she has

Is mature

Is happy

Has a natural affinity for her

Is growing emotionally and spiritually

Likes life and enjoys the world

Likes to learn about things

Is kind

Is inquisitive

Is friendly

Wants to have a loving extended family

Fits with her family

Helps her feel secure emotionally and financially

Wants to make a warm home with her

Likes to have friends over to enjoy the home they have created together

Is healthy and wants to stay healthy

Enjoys traveling

Likes exploring, sightseeing, painting, dancing, and sharing

Makes her feel safe in the world

Shares her spiritual beliefs

Has lots of interests, yet has time for travel and fun adventures

Is caring

Has a good sense of humor

Is giving

Likes to communicate

Is experimental sexually

Is expressive

Is romantic

Is a dreamer

Is intelligent

Is a rational thinker

Is a good negotiator

Is financially secure

Loves music

Plays tennis

Rides bikes

Scuba dives

Is a good dancer

Likes to go to the gym

Likes to take aerobic classes

Has healed his relationship with his parents

Is connected

Is intimate

Is cozy

Likes a variety in sexual expression

Looks sexy

Moves gracefully

Is comfortable with his body

Is attentive

Lets her know he loves her

Is confident around her

Is comfortable to be with

Has a similar history to her

Relates to the world like she does

Has similar values

Gets along with her friends, and she get along with his friends

Is her friend

Has a creative active mind

Is streetwise

Thinks she is smart

Wants to know what she thinks about things

Is self-sufficient

Likes helping out around the house

Loves children

Loves animals

Loves nature

WHAT SOME MEN WANT

A woman who: Has desire

Is adventurous

Is giving

Is respectful

Likes sex

Makes her own money

Is warm

Has a natural affinity for him

Is growing emotionally and spiritually

Is generous

Is quiet

Reads current events

Is intuitive

Likes her body

Takes care of her body

Is artistic

Is flexible

Is compassionate

Is sexy

Is self-sufficient

Is articulate

Is an animal lover

Is aware of nature

Has a willingness to explore sexuality

Is able to identify and share things she likes and dislikes

Has pretty eyes

Has a nice smile with good teeth

Has a willingness to open her heart

Expresses her pain and her good feelings

Is able to see his point of view and is willing to negotiate

Has good self-esteem

Is athletic

Enjoys arts and leisure

Likes to travel and take vacations

Shares his faith or spiritual beliefs

Wants to raise a family with mutual beliefs and values

Has a strong, loving, and supportive family

Gets along and accepts his family despite their shortcomings

Wants to prosper, yet doesn't have to have a lot of money

Has a career

Knows how to make money

Is frugal but not cheap

Is a companion

Is a friend

Is open-minded

Is intelligent

Is loving

Is caring

Is sensual

Is fun

Is a partner

Is sexually creative

Is creative

Loves the outdoors

Is a travel companion

Loves movies

Loves to eat and cook

Loves to have him cook for her

Loves herself

Is comfortable with her own looks

Is stimulating intellectually

Loves to fly

Allows him to explore his hobbies and interests

Is musical

Is not overly clean

Is very clean and orderly

Is spiritual but not involved in any one religion

Doesn't wear underwear

Has a good sense of humor

FIVE LOVE CHANNELS

Gary Chapman wrote a book titled *The Five Love Languages*. In the book, he describes the various ways partners attempt to give and receive love. The information below is a synopsis of his book. If you want more information about his work, you can always go to the source.

There are basically five primary ways or channels we give and receive love. We give on all five channels, and we want to receive on all five. However, we all seem to have a primary channel that just seems to ring our bell. If our partner, boss, or friend is not delivering on our primary channel, we will often feel unloved and our "love bucket" will eventually run dry. It is at this point that we start to look someplace else for our loving. We change partners, find a new job with an understanding boss, seek a new friend, or seek some other source like food, drugs, alcohol, gambling, or sex. If we know what our primary love channel is and what it is for those we care about, we can consciously ask for what works for us and give to them what works for them.

The five love channels are Quality Time, Words of Appreciation, Acts of Service, Gifts, and Touching.

If my primary love channel is Quality Time, then I need to have you sit in front of me and talk to me, and I want you to listen to me. I just want to be with you and have us share our worlds.

If my primary love channel is Words of Appreciation, then I need you to tell me how wonderful I am, that you love me, and that you think I am smart, attractive, and all the other positive qualities you find in me.

If my primary love channel is Acts of Service, then I need you to help me around the house, to take out the trash, to fold the clothes, to wash the car, and to help me with all the little day-to-day tasks.

If my primary love channel is Gifts, then I need you to give me little things that show me you care. It could be a rock you found, some flowers you saw, a picture you drew, a note or poem you wrote, or a cup of coffee. The cost of the item you give me it not important. It's your giving me an item that I can look at, hold, and treasure that's important.

If my primary love channel is Touching, then I need you to touch me, to hold me, to kiss me, to sit close to me, to make love to me, or just to hold my hand. I just need to feel your touch.

If you are in a relationship and you feel unloved by your partner and your partner feels confused because s/he feels s/he is giving lots of love, I suspect your primary love channel is not being fulfilled.

We often give what we want to receive. If my primary love channel is Words of Appreciation, then I would tell my partner how wonderful she is all the time. If her primary love channel is Acts of Service, then she would be doing all kinds of little things for me. I would appreciate all she does—it's nice that she does all that stuff—but she never tells me how wonderful I am, and I just do not think she loves me that much because she is not filling me through my primary love channel. I, of course, do not do many things for her. Why should I? She is so self-sufficient. Therefore, she doesn't feel I love her all that much. I say nice things, but I don't do much. Both of us are saying "I love you" in our own way, but no one is hearing it and we both feel empty. I therefore do less around the house, she says fewer words of appreciation, and we are left feeling unloved, unheard, unappreciated, rejected, and empty.

There are three ways to discover your primary love channel.

1.   What does your partner do or fail to do that hurts you deeply? The opposite of what hurts you most is probably your primary love channel.

2.   What have you most often requested of your partner? The thing you have most often requested is likely your primary love channel.

3.   How do you regularly express love to your partner? Your method of expressing love could be indicative of your primary love channel.

Love is a choice. We can request things from our partners, but we cannot demand things. Criticism and demands drive wedges. We decide daily to love or not to love our partner. If we choose to love, then expressing it in the way our partner needs or requests is easy. If we are wise, we can transform our partner's criticisms into requests. People tend to criticize most loudly in the area where they have the deepest emotional need. Criticisms often need clarification. Criticizing is an ineffective way of pleading for love; however, it might be the only way our partner knows how to request a change. If we choose, we can learn to give our love to our partner in a way that is effective and in a way that they can receive.

There is an old saying that applies here. "If you like the results you have, then keep doing what you're doing. If, however, you want different results, then you will have to do something different." What you do differently or what is effective is determined by the results. If the results are what you want, then your method is effective. As I suggested earlier in Chapter 3, I am not so concerned with the method. I am focused on fulfilling the intention. If I want a loving and joy-filled relationship, I will do what it takes to create loving and joy.

REQUEST FOR CHANGE

This brings us to an interesting place. Let's assume I don't like what is happening in my relationship with you, and I want it to be different. My intention is to create that loving and joy-filled relationship with you, so how do I get it? How do I create change in me and you to fulfill my intention?

I have observed an interesting phenomenon: anytime I ask you, myself, my child, my employee, my friend, a stranger, or whomever to change or to do something different, I run into resistance. People resist requests for change for two primary reasons. We as humans resist requests for change out of fear or because of denial.

Fear says, "That's scary. I don't know how to do that. I have never done that before. I don't know what would happen if I did that. I don't know what my life would be like. I don't like doing unfamiliar things. I want to do it my way, the way I have always done it. The way I am familiar with."

Denial says, "That's not my problem. That's your problem. I am doing it the right way. That is the wrong way. I am fine just the way I am. This is your issue, not mine. I like the way I do it, and I am not changing."

The response to a request for change is anger or hurt feelings. Remember anger and hurt feelings are tools we use to get people to do what we want. "I want you to accept me the way I am. If you loved me, you would just learn to live with my little quirks. I am angry at you for not accepting me, and I am not going to change."

We continue to request changes, and now we begin to argue and fight. Eventually, we are fighting all the time. Then we begin withdrawing our love from each other. This is how that couple you see sitting in a restaurant not talking to each other got there. You know that when they first met they were talking and listening to each other with love in their eyes and ears. Everything was just fine. No one needed to do anything different.

Then, in time, someone asked for a change, and resistance occurred because of fear or denial, and they responded with anger or hurt feelings. Time continues to pass until they arrive at the point where they fight about this and fight about that and fight about this again, until eventually they say to each other, silently or nonverbally, "I'm not talking to you. Every time we talk you criticize me, you make me wrong, and you fight with me. I have nothing to say to you." Ouch. And their intention was to create a loving and joy-filled relationship. What a sad story. Most people are fighting to get love.

From my point of view, this is not an effective approach. However, it's what most of us do and, as I suggested, it doesn't matter who we ask. It just doesn't matter. This is another one of those areas I would ask you to check out for yourself. Go ask people to do something different, to correct their behavior, and watch what they do. Ask yourself to do something different and watch what you do.

If all this is true, then how do we get ourselves and/or others to do things differently without going through the anger or hurt feelings before the withdrawing of love?

What I am going to suggest may seem very obvious and very simplistic, and it is. Unfortunately, very few people know how to do it, or know how to do it effectively, and thus they give up and go back to their old, punishing pattern of requesting change and end up fighting.

We must first be aware of what we want. You say, "I know what I want. I want my husband to stop chewing with his mouth open, and I hate it when he licks his fingers when he eats chicken. That's what I want!" My response is, "No, that is not what you want. That is what you don't want."

Here is where many people get disappointed and discouraged. Earlier, we said we get what we focus on and that our basic self only hears the last few things we say. So, if you say, "Stop chewing with your mouth open," he hears "mouth open." Or if you say "I hate it when you lick your fingers," he hears, "lick fingers." So your husband keeps chewing with his mouth open and licking his fingers, and you get angrier and angrier. You keep focusing on him chewing with his mouth open. You watch and wait for him to put his fingers in his mouth so you can scold him. Eventually he no longer wants to dine with you. You wonder why.

What you really want is your husband to chew with his mouth closed and to use a napkin to wipe the sauce off his fingers when he eats barbeque chicken. So your request for change could sound like, "Please chew with your mouth closed, and use a napkin to wipe the sauce off your fingers." Now we have a clear request and a goal. He knows what you want. He knows the end result that will make you happy. Wonderful!

Now, I'm not a fool. I don't expect him to change his behavior just because you asked him in a clear, direct way. I know he has been chomping and licking long before you came into his life. This is an old pattern that is deeply ingrained in his unconscious. Changing a pattern here is not necessarily an easy or fast thing to do. So what do you do? Beat him with a spoon? No, you give him one of the four things we are all starved for each time he moves towards the requested change. When his behavior approximates the change you want, give him approval, appreciation, attention, and/or love. We are all staved for these four things. As he slowly moves toward the goal or the requested behavior, you reward him with approval, appreciation, attention, and/or love, and in time, change occurs.

Most people withhold the reward until the goal has been achieved. This is not an effective approach. It is more effective if you give the reward along the way. If your husband is starting out at point A, then you give him a reward at point B. If you wait until he gets to point Z, well, getting to point Z just might not ever occur.

What does this sound like? you ask.

Using the example above with the chomping and licking husband, you would want to catch your husband chewing with his mouth closed and using a napkin to wipe his fingers. When you notice that he is honoring your request, you could say, "It makes me so proud that you are honoring my request. Thank you. I love you for listening to me." Or you could touch him and just give him a loving smile or offer any other words of appreciation that are appropriate.

You say, "This is a lot of work! He should just be able to change. He's a big boy. He should know better by now. I am not going to treat him like a baby. I'm not his mother. I don't want to do all of that. It takes too much energy. Besides, this is a simple thing. It won't work with something real or something serious. I just don't have the time for such nonsense."

I hear you. As I said when I began this section, this will sound very simplistic and simple. However, what I am suggesting is very challenging to do and very effective. If you reread the statements above, you will see a lot of "shoulds," a lot of judgments, and a lot of unexpressed anger. And I suspect with that approach, love will be withdrawn and separation will occur. It becomes a choice in how you want to go through life. We can go through life seeing everything that is not working our way, or we can go through life with enthusiasm as we watch ourselves and others learning and growing as we go through time.

If we give others and ourselves those four things we are all starved for—approval, appreciation, attention and/or love—we will have people around us with smiles on their faces and joy in their hearts, and we will be getting more of what we want from them. Check it out.

REQUEST FOR CHANGE

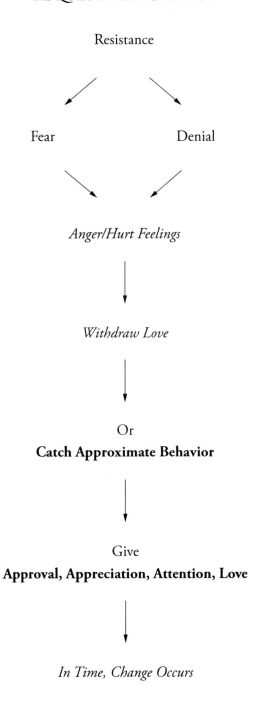

Resistance

Fear   Denial

Anger/Hurt Feelings

Withdraw Love

Or
Catch Approximate Behavior

Give
Approval, Appreciation, Attention, Love

In Time, Change Occurs

LISTENING

When I ask you to listen to me

and you start giving advice,

you have not done what I asked.

When I ask you to listen to me

and you begin to tell me why I shouldn't feel

that way, you are trampling on my feelings.

When I ask you to listen to me

and you feel you have to do something to

solve my problems, you have failed me,

strange as that may seem.

Listen! All I asked was that you listen,

not talk or do—just hear me.

Advice is cheap: 25 cents will get you both Dear Abby

and Billy Graham in the same newspaper.

And I can do for myself. I'm not helpless.

Maybe discouraged and faltering, but not helpless.

When you do something for me that I can and need

to do for myself, you contribute to my fear

and inadequacy.

But when you accept as a simple fact that I do

feel what I feel, no matter how irrational,

then I can quit trying to convince you and can

get about the business of understanding what's

behind this irrational feeling.

And when that's clear, the answers are

obvious and I don't need advice.

Irrational feelings make sense when we understand

what's behind them.

Perhaps that's why prayer works, sometimes, for some

people—because God is mute, and S/he doesn't give

advice or try to fix things. "They" just listen

and let you work it out for yourself.

So please listen and just hear me. And, if you want to

talk, wait a minute for your turn, and I'll listen to you.

By Ralph Roughton, M.D.

LEVELS OF COMMUNICATION

How do I talk to you so you can hear what I'm saying? Can you see what I'm showing you? Can you feel me groping for words for you to grasp?

Communication is a challenge on many levels. We send information in a certain form to another person, and they receive it. Many times something along the way is lost and miscommunication, hurt feelings, or anger become the byproducts.

You ask, "What happened? Did I say the wrong thing?" The answer just might be yes.

We must first realize that anytime we say anything to anyone, we are generalizing, deleting, or distorting information. In fact, as I'm telling you this, I'm generalizing, deleting, and distorting information. Do you know what it's called when we generalize, delete, or distort information? It's called lying. And we have all heard the old saying, "We can live with anyone except a liar," and yet, we are lying to one another all the time. What a predicament to be in.

If it's true that we are always generalizing, deleting, or distorting information, and all evidence seems to indicate that this is so, then how can we ever trust anybody, or even ourselves for that matter? How can we communicate anything to anybody without putting our foot in our mouth, somewhere, sometime? The answer is, you can't. Sorry. Life just is not fair. It just does what it does and people do what they do, and miscommunications are part of being human.

"OK. I got your point. Maybe I should just keep my mouth shut and not say anything."

In some ways, there's a lot of wisdom in that. However, humans do like to communicate, and all the miscommunications can make life more exciting.

"I am not into that kind of excitement," you say. "Isn't there a way to be better communicators?"

"Yes." Notice I generalized, deleted, and distorted information with my answer?

Yes, there are things we can do to improve our communication with ourselves and with others. Besides being aware that we are generalizing, deleting, and distorting information, it is helpful to be aware that humans communicate on three basic levels. We communicate in visual terms, in auditory terms, and in kinesthetic or feeling terms. To make communication more exciting, it is helpful to know that we actually use all three levels. Some of us prefer, however, to communicate in visual terms, while others prefer auditory or kinesthetic terms. This is where communication can break down very quickly.

For example, if I am a visual person and you are a kinesthetic person, we would probably have a lot of miscommunication. Many couples experience a lot of miscommunication because they communicate in different terms.

Let's say a woman is primarily a visual person and her husband is primarily a kinesthetic person. It is midweek and she wants to create a special evening with her husband, so she begins by making the house *look* pretty. She gets flowers and cleans everything till it shines and everything *looks* nice. She then proceeds to make herself *look* pretty, putting on a colorful dress and fixing her hair and make-up. She *looks* beautiful. Her husband comes home, and he *feels* that something is up. He *feels* movement inside himself and grabs his wife, and without saying anything to her begins to paw her. She breaks away angrily and says, "That is all you ever think about. You never tell me how nice I *look* or anything." He walks away *feeling* totally confused and angry that she doesn't appreciate his *touching*, which is his way of expressing the affection he has for her.

What we really have here are two people speaking different languages. In the above case, if the husband used more visual words in his communication, his wife would begin to see his affection for her. At the same time, if the wife used more kinesthetic means, her husband would feel more loved and appreciated.

The above example is a simplistic model of how we are often misunderstood and how we can move toward better communication. It is important to remember that we all use visual, verbal, and kinesthetic terms in our communication and that we all have a primary mode. If we know what our primary mode is and what the primary mode is of the person we are communicating with, we can adjust our language and have better communication. If you listen to the words you speak or the words of others, it becomes pretty obvious what our primary mode is. The following chart lists some of the words in each mode.

Visual	Auditory	Kinesthetic
Appear	Accent	Caress
Bright	Address	Carry
Clarify	Amplify	Contact
Clear	Ask	Crash
Delineate	Click	Embrace
Expose	Compose	Grab
Focus	Discourse	Grasp
Glance	Growl	Grip
Look	Harmonize	Hammer
Outlook	Hear	Handle
Peek	Lecture	Hit
Perspective	Listen	Hold
Picture	Loud	Impress
Preview	Muffle	Move
Reveal	Music	Rub
Screen	Noise	Sharp
See	Pitch	Shock
Show	Preach	Smooth

Sight	Rattle	Sore
Spectacle	Ring	Squeeze
Spot	Say	Stir
View	Scream	Tap
Vision	Shout	Taste
Visualize	Speak	Throw
Watch	Tell	Tickle

ACTIVE LISTENING

Now that you are aware that people speak in three basic formats and you realize the importance of listening, the question that comes up most often is, "How do I listen effectively?"

Listening is a powerful skill that is learned. It requires practice, practice, and more practice. There are two things people do if they don't feel they are being heard. They will repeat themselves over and over, and/or they will raise their voice. Many people hold an erroneous belief: if I yell at you, then you will hear me. This, of course, often is not the case. In fact, most people shut down and stop listening when they are being yelled at. However, it's nice to be able to realize when people don't feel they are not being heard. As I suggested, they will start yelling or repeating themselves. If this happens, it is a clear indication for you to do some active listening. If you find that you are repeating yourself to someone or yelling at them, then you probably don't think they are hearing you either. You could ask them to do some active listening.

So what is active listening?

Active listening is a therapeutic tool that has been around for a very long time. Basically, I tell you what I heard you say. I use your words as closely as possible. I don't interpret your words; I use your words. This helps us speak in the same language, whether it is visual, auditory, or kinesthetic. This can feel like I am just parroting you or mimicking you, but I'm not.

I am just repeating your words, and you will feel like I am finally hearing you. When I repeat your words, it doesn't mean I agree with you or disagree with you. It just means that I hear what you are saying. Once you are clear that I hear what you are saying on the surface level, then you can drop to the next level, and then the next level, until eventually you are telling me what you really want to tell me. You couldn't tell me the deeper message until you knew I heard the surface message. Without active listening, you would not feel heard. You would feel you would have to argue with me to prove your point so that I would agree with you. When I am actively listening, you don't have to convince me of anything. I don't have to prove you wrong or make you hear my point; I just listen. I am not making any commitments to you. I am just listening.

As we go through this process of active listening, it is valuable to speak in short phrases rather than long paragraphs. This keeps us current with each other. We will know what we have said to each other. We will know what has been heard. Most people, particularly when they are arguing with each other, speak in paragraph form and go on and on. Their partner responds, reacts, or defends against the last thing spoken. Their rebuttal is also in paragraph form, and they go on and on. Their partner does the same, and a downward spiral of miscommunication and misunderstanding happens, leaving everyone walking away unfulfilled, exhausted, and defeated. Because most of what has been spoken was not responded to, everyone feels unheard, and yes, now they have to repeat themselves and/ or yell at each other some more. Ugh! I'd say this type of communication is not very effective. However, if we speak in short phrases and repeat what we have heard using each others' words, we will know that everything has been heard correctly. As a result, repetition and yelling decreases, and we can move toward creating a win-win solution.

This can be a very tedious process, and I wouldn't ask you to do it for more than about ten or fifteen minutes at a time. And of course, you don't have to do this with all of your communication. It is just during those challenging or sensitive times that it is necessary, or when you find you are repeating yourself or raising your voice.

In the communication process, I put the responsibility on both sides of the fence. This means that if I find myself repeating myself or raising my voice, I can ask you what you heard me say. Or if you are repeating yourself or raising your voice, I can drop into the active listening process and tell you what I am hearing you say. The responsibility for clear communication is with everyone involved.

People usually get into trouble or miscommunication when they make assumptions. The definition of assuming is in the spelling. Anytime we assume something, we make an "ass" out of "u" and "me." Making things even more challenging and confusing is that most people assume against themselves. They lose in their fantasies. They have negative self-talk. They forget their partner is on their side. They forget that their partner is their ally.

Most primary relationships have a few unstated agreements. The agreements are as follows: We love each other, and we won't consciously do anything to hurt each other. We are a team, and we are here to work together. We will watch each other's backs and protect each other. The primary intention to each other is not to hurt each other but to create a relationship where love and peace can exist and flourish.

If this is true, then how do people get into arguments in which they hurt each other?

If you watch and listen, you will see and hear most arguments occur when someone has made an erroneous assumption. Because of their erroneous assumption, their partner reacts in a defensive manner. They feel they need to defend themselves against the assumed attack. They move into a position of "rightness" and attempt to force their partner to see their point of view. Their partner feels attacked and often insulted and feels they have to attack back. Now both are arguing from their position of "rightness." Hurtful words are said, and more defending and attacking occurs. Eventually, one partner will overpower the other and "win" the argument, or both partners will become exhausted and temporarily retreat. After a time of cooling off, they remember that they love each other. They don't like the feeling of separation and soon wonder, "What were we fighting about?" They make up, and all is forgiven. A bandage is placed over the gaping wound, and life goes on—that is, until down the road another erroneous assumption is made and another fight begins and on and on. Eventually, the couple withdraws their love from each other, and in time separation occurs.

Is there another way? you ask. Yes, there certainly is. However, it does require change. In couples therapy, the first statement I often make is, "If you like the results you have in your relationship, then keep doing what you are doing. If you want different results, then you will have to do something different. What that difference is we will find out." This is where the concept of "intention verses method" shows up. As I said earlier, I am not attached to the method; I am, however, focused on the intention of creating a loving, peaceful relationship.

What to do differently? There are so many things that it's hard to begin. Let's look at the situation above and see what could be done differently to create love and peace in that relationship.

One thing a couple can do is what I call a perception check. A perception check is a communication process in which we check our perceptions or our assumptions. Basically, we ask our partner what they meant by their statement or what the intention was behind their statement. This could sound like, "That comment made me feel like a bad child. Were you attempting to make me feel stupid? Were you trying to teach me a lesson? Were you attacking me? Was your intention to hurt me and make me feel wrong or bad? Were you trying to hurt me or punish me?"

For the most part, I have found that people are attempting to get their partner to do "it," whatever that is, the "right" way. The right way of doing "it" is usually their way. They want their partner to be safe in the world and not to get hurt, or to look stupid to others, so they will correct or parent their partner the way they were corrected or parented as a child. Often, the correcting or parenting process is very dysfunctional and ineffective. However, it is how their parents corrected them and how their parents loved them, and because they love their partner, they correct their partner the way they were corrected.

By doing a perception check, you often find that the intention of the communication was not to hurt but rather to keep your partner from being hurt or from doing something "wrong," where hurt on some level would occur.

Isn't it strange? We hurt the person we love as a way of keeping them from being hurt.

By doing a perception check, we often discover that we misunderstood our partner; we assumed they were out to get us, and thus we felt we needed to strike back at them. We could also do some active listening as a way of really listening to what is being said. Active listening is another way to avoid assuming what is being said. With clear, active, and accurate communication, most people are able to work together as a unit and stay in a loving, peaceful place.

Working together as a unit is a key to a healthy, long-term relationship. However, this often brings up the issue of control. I frequently hear people say, "He always wants to do it his way" or "She always wants to be in control and do it her way." The truth is that we all want to be in control all of the time. In truth, it isn't an issue of control; it's an issue of direction. In order to understand this further, let's explore the concept of direction.

AN ISSUE OF CONTROL OR DIRECTION

I would like you to imagine two people facing each other, holding their right hands together like people do when they are shaking hands. Standing looking at each other, the statement, "You are in charge and in control," is made to the person on the right by a third party. The same statement, "You are in charge and in control is also told to the person on the left. They are then both instructed to walk in opposite directions. A tug of war begins. Who wins? The person who is either physically or verbally the strongest wins the game. The loser feels ashamed and loses an aspect of him- or herself, as s/he is forced to surrender under the power of the other. Sound familiar? This process is not fun in relationships, although it is what most of us do. So let's try another approach.

Now imagine two people standing next to each other. They are holding hands and facing in the same direction. The statement "You are in charge and in control" is told to both people. They are instructed to walk in the same direction, basically at the same speed. A nice, peaceful movement occurs. No one loses. No one feels ashamed. No one is hurt. Cooperation has occurred, and both maintained their own individuality and control. Love and peace are present.

With this demonstration, it becomes obvious that the issue is not one of control; it's an issue of direction. If both people are moving in the same direction at basically the same speed, everyone can maintain his or her own identity.

What is important here is that both people have an agreed goal or "mission statement." I have discovered that most couples do not have a mission statement. When asked, "Why are you two together?" the answer is, "Well, we love each other." That's nice, but often that is not enough. Loving is extremely important. It's a key element, but more is often required.

In the olden days, in couples therapy, couples were told that they just simply needed to learn how to compromise. When people compromise, they give up some of what they want and the other person has to give up some of what they want. From my point of view, this is a lose-lose situation. No one is really happy, resentment repeatedly builds up, and sooner or later another argument shows up over the same issue. Somewhere in the 1970s, the concept of win-win showed up, and then in the 1980s and 1990s, we started to hear the concepts of "mission statements" and "consensus."

What was that all about?

Basically, it's been discovered that if we can get people to agree on a mission statement, to come into a consensus, meaning that everyone is in agreement, then everyone could maintain a sense of personal identity and personal control while moving together with others to fulfill a common goal. Then, the concept began to be applied to our primary relationships, to our families, and to our local communities as a way of creating peace and harmony.

A mission statement is a statement of values, a direction, a reason, or a purpose for being together and for being alive on Planet Earth. It is extremely valuable for a couple to create a mission statement together. It gives them a direction to walk toward. It helps to set the intention in the relationship. It also gives them a way out of most misunderstandings or arguments.

Let's say a couple's mission statement is, "To grow, to be the best we can be, to support each other in our personal and professional goals, to learn to love, to learn to communicate better, to heal the wounds of the past, to create peace in our lives and others, to create and share our abundance with each other and our loved ones, and to grow a healthy family."

If this couple has a disagreement, one thing they can do is look at their mission statement and identify where they are off course. The situation might be a mirror of something in the past. and they could use the disturbance as a way of looking at a past issue with fresh eyes. This could bring in the quality of compassion and understanding for the action that has caused the disturbance. Or it could be a place where they could learn to communicate clearer, to do some active listening or perception checking. The disturbance becomes an opportunity for growth and expansion rather than a place of wounding, top-dogging, or shaming. By using their mission statement, the couple can move back to a position of loving.

The couple could also decide that this situation is one of those times when they just disagree. Having a primary agreement that it's OK to disagree can be a powerful and effective key to help you get back into the loving.

There are two wonderful questions to keep asking in your relationship. If all is going well and you are getting the results you want, then ask, "How do we stay in the loving?" You are doing things that are effective, and it is a good idea to be conscious of what those things are so you can keep doing them. If however, you are having a challenging moment, you could ask, "How do we get back into the loving?" The answer to this question will give a positive direction out of the painful situation into a positive, uplifting, and loving direction.

HOW TO HAVE A HOUSE MEETING

Many relationships have something I call "old business" that sits between two people, blocking their communication and their loving. Old business is something that is unresolved. It could be something that was said or an action that was taken. It could be a huge issue, or it could be something small that just keeps popping up and you don't know how to discuss it. In time, the old business pot gets full until there is an eruption of sorts, allowing everyone to speak his or her truth. In a healthy relationship, the issues get resolved and the couple can return to their loving. In an unhealthy relationship, words are said and actions are taken that can create more and more of a separation between the partners. In order to avoid these types of disturbances, it is a wise idea to have regular house meetings before an eruption occurs.

There are a few ground rules to creating a successful house meeting. It is important to limit the time of the meeting. You do not want a three- or four-hour marathon session. That would be way too much for most people.

So set a timer for thirty to forty minutes. That's it. You probably will end the meeting feeling unfinished. That's OK. It will motivate you to set up another meeting in the near future at which you can reconsider the issues. This gives you time to process what you have discussed and you just might come up with a new perspective by the time you return to the issue. It is important to remember that a relationship is an ongoing process. There really isn't an end to the process. A house meeting once a month is a good starting point for a relationship that is working. If you are in a relationship with many unresolved issues, then once a week, or every other week, might be more appropriate.

It is important to emphasize that the meeting is to create a positive experience. There might be some upset and some misunderstanding, so be gentle with yourself and your partner. You are having this house meeting as a way to create more love and understanding. Your intention is to discover what is working and what is not working, to take some course corrections in order to create a win-win situation.

Having a special object to pass back and forth is a nice ritual to incorporate. The object can be anything that reminds you of or brings you back to a loving place. Whoever is holding the object is the one who gets to speak. The other person gets to listen. This allows you to say what you want to say without the fear of being interrupted. This is also a time when active listening can be implemented if confusion or some misunderstanding occurs. Even though the intent of the house meeting is to create more loving in the relationship, some type of upset can occur. By doing the active listening process, you will often be able to understand what your partner is saying.

You can use a couple of statements to help prime the pump. The first one is, "I want more of ..." The second is, "I want less of ..." These two statements will often help direct you to what is or is not working in your relationship. It is important to note that there are a few things that we always want more of even though we are getting them. For example, you could say, "I want more kissing in our relationship." And your partner could say, "I kiss you." You respond by saying, "Yes, and I love the way you kiss me and I want more." What I am suggesting here is that just because your partner is asking for more of something doesn't mean you are doing anything wrong; it just means they want more.

In your house meeting, you want to bring up your issues or those things that are disturbing to you as well as those things that are positive, the things that give you joy. In your sharing, you want to speak from your point of view, using "I" and not "you." For example, you say, "I want more kissing in the morning," not "You never kiss me in the morning."

As you have your house meetings, be open to revise how they are structured. Are they frequent enough, too long, not positive enough? Do you want to change the structure or the content in some way? Create what works for you and your partner.

HOW TO CREATE A MISSION STATEMENT

Creating a mission statement can be fun and exciting. It is an opportunity to explore and discover what is important to you and to share this sacred information with someone you love, someone you want to share your life with. It can also be challenging and scary for some people. Some of us haven't really been given permission to ask for what we want. If these folks are asked, "What do you want?" their response often is, "I don't know. What do you want?" If this is who you are, then writing down your values, your goals, and your wants can feel like walking through a wall. I would just ask you to be gentle with yourself. Know we are not carving this statement into granite. The statement can be changed and updated as time passes. In fact, it is wise to revisit your mission statement regularly to see if it is still accurate. We as humans grow and change through time; therefore, our values, goals, and wants often change as well. Know that creating a mission statement is an ongoing process.

With a sense of freedom and an eraser in hand, write down a bunch of adjectives and adverbs that describe what you want. For example, you could write, "I want love, peace, joy, health, happiness, abundance, growth, excitement, adventure, learning, understanding, healing, and laughter." The list can be as long as you like. There really are no rules here. Let your creativity have a good time. As you are writing your list, your partner could be writing his or her list as well.

Now sit down together and share your lists. What things are the same? Write these things down. What things or qualities include or encompass other qualities? In the list above, you see "excitement" and "adventure." You might feel they are the same and that with adventure comes excitement or vice versa. You might want to choose between the two words, or you might want both of them written down because they have different meanings to you.

As you join your list with your partner's, you will have a long run-on sentence. This is fine. You might want to shorten it, or you just might like the long version. Whatever the two of you both like is what we are looking for. This is called coming to a consensus. There is no rush here. Enjoy the process. Communication is taking place in a very special way about some very special things. You are essentially setting the foundation for your relationship. You are creating a direction that both of you want to go in.

Once you are happy with your mission statement, write it out and hang it on your refrigerator or bathroom mirror, where you can both look at it and "live" with it for a while. After a week or two, take it down and read it to each other. Do you want to make any changes? How do you feel when you read it out loud now? Make any revisions you both feel are needed, and then hang the revised copy back up and read it regularly. Use it if a disagreement arises. Ask the question, "How can we use our mission statement as a way to resolve this disagreement?" Or "How can I change my point of view so I can be in alignment with our mission statement?"

RELATIONSHIPS ARE CLASSROOMS

From my point of view, relationships are classrooms. You enter into a classroom to learn something. When you have learned what it is that you are to learn, you get to graduate. Some classes last a lifetime, while some last a night. They all have value. If you have learned one thing about yourself or life, then the class has been a success. Many people have been programmed to think that the class is a failure if it doesn't last a lifetime. Therefore, they walk around with a history of failed classes or failed relationships. I just cannot accept this point of view. I remember who my first girlfriend was in the first grade. I remember going to her house and giving her a gift for her birthday. It was a big deal. I learned a lot in that relationship. I learned to walk through some fears. I learned there were people around me who were wiser than me, my parents, who could encourage me to step into what I wanted and who taught me manners and respect. I learned a lot. I'm not with that little girl today. I have no idea where she is or what she is doing. I could chalk that up as a failure because I'm not with her.

This might seem like an absurd example, and it is; however, it is as absurd as labeling any other relationship I've walked through as a failure. I have grown and learned how to have a relationship by being in relationships. Some lasted longer than others, some ended more smoothly than others, and with each one there was learning. Each one was a successful relationship. I have grown. I have learned to communicate. I have learned what I want and how to ask for it in an effective, loving way. I have laughed, I have cried, I have been angry, I have experienced joy, and I have experienced bliss.

You might say, "That's nice, but I've had some terrible relationships in the past. I have really been hurt. I've been abandoned, betrayed, and abused. I can't see how I could call these relationships successful. They were failures. I got a divorce. That hurt like hell. I felt ashamed, and I felt like a failure. My partner had an affair, and my guts were ripped out of me and stomped on. That doesn't feel like a successful relationship. I was in a battering relationship with an alcoholic, and things happened to me and my children that I can't bear to think about. I was a fool to stay so long. No success there. What are you talking about?"

Yes, all of those things, and much more, happen to us when we are in relationships. Things happen that are challenging for everyone involved. This is where all the stuff earlier in this book comes into play. We first give ourselves permission to express our anger and rage with the writing, burning or tearing, and holding on exercise. Then, we work with the process of acceptance and move into the process of forgiveness. After forgiving, we do the healing of memories exercise. It is here that the deeper work takes place. This is where the wise one inside of us shows up and assists us in learning from our past. While we are in the middle of the struggle, it is challenging to see the learning. Often, it is only after we have gained some time and space that we can claim the success or learning from a painful relationship.

RELATIONSHIPS ARE LIKE SWIMMING POOLS

It's a hot day. There's a swimming pool. If you get into the pool, will it be a good experience?

It seems like it. Will it? You don't really know. So you put your big toe in the water. Hmm. Not bad. You put your foot in, and now you are in water up to your ankle. It seems all right thus far. You wade in a little farther, and you are now in water up to your knees. It feels good. Slowly, you keep going, and you are now in water up to your waist. A major decision and a commitment have been made. Still seems OK. Now you're swimming around. It's refreshing. Ah, good. You feel confident that you made the right decision by getting in the pool. After swimming around for a while, you realize that your eyes are burning. Oh no. There is too much chlorine in the water. You have to get out because it is just too painful to stay in the water.

Was it a bad decision to get into the pool? I don't think so. Sometimes you really don't know if something will work for you until after you have experienced it. You can't tell until you get involved and enmeshed on some level. Some pools have dark, murky water and snakes swimming in them. Those are pretty obvious for the most part; others, however, can look pretty good. Determining whether the ones that look good work for you can initially be challenging. Making this decision often requires you to become involved. If you get involved, you might discover that there is too much chlorine in the water. This does not mean you made a bad decision, that you are a failure and can't trust your decision making process. It just means that you are participating in your life.

Getting involved in a relationship is very much like checking out that swimming pool. It can look very good and exciting initially. It seems to call you. What will you experience? How long will it last? It's hard to say. I'm sure you will learn something. Is it wise to get involved? Sometimes it's wise to walk down the street to another pool, but sometimes you will have to check it out and discover what there is to learn. If there is too much pain and struggle, then it is wise to complete the relationship, to say goodbye.

SAYING GOODBYE

How do you say goodbye in a healthy way? It is one of those things that we pretend we will not have to do. However, as I stated earlier, one of four things will happen in any relationship you get involved in: you will leave, they will leave, they will die, or you will die. That means that somewhere in time, even in the best of relationships, we have to say goodbye. Unfortunately, most of us do not know how to say goodbye, and we often do it in a very hurtful or dysfunctional manner. On the other hand, there is a way of saying goodbye that can be very loving and can leave you and the other person feeling complete and intact.

With saying goodbye, we will experience the process of grief. It is also just a part of being in a relationship. Sometimes we avoid intimate relationships because of our fear of experiencing the "discomfort" of grief. Unfortunately, grief just seems to be a part of the process of life. Things come and go, and people come and go. As I suggested earlier, change seems to be one of those things that is constant in our lives. Because loss is a part of life, it's best to embrace it rather than be in denial. So let's explore the process of grief.

There are basically five stages in the process of grief. They are denial, anger, bargaining, depression, and acceptance.

Denial is when we say, "I can't believe this is happening to me. I can't believe they said that or that they did that. I can't believe it." We feel numb inside. Our mind is a blur. We are in a state of shock.

When we start to become aware and as we come out of our shock, we feel angry. We are angry at them for what they did or didn't do. We are angry at ourselves for not seeing the signs. We are angry at God. We are angry at the person in the car next to us. We are just angry at the world. We feel life just isn't fair.

Then we shift into the bargaining phase. In this phase, we rethink everything. We think that if they hadn't or if we hadn't or if they had said or done it differently or if we had said or done it differently, then the results would be different. We would still be together. Our mind races through the past and into the future. All sorts of scenarios pass through our minds. We think we are going crazy trying to figure it out and trying to create a different ending.

Somewhere in here, we drop into depression. Depression with grief is different from "normal" depression. It just comes out of nowhere. It's like the floor falls out from under you. You find yourself looking out into space with no energy, no desire, and no will to do anything but to just sit or lie there. Life feels pointless. Then, in the next moment, you are up and about; then you are down again, then up, then down. You feel like you are on some wild roller coaster ride with no end in sight.

Then you come to a place of acceptance. "Yes, they are gone. Yes, I am alone. It's over. I have been here before. I know what to do. I will make it." A momentary sense of peace floods over you. A sense of calm is present.

It would be nice if you had to go through these five stages only once. Unfortunately, it doesn't work that way. You get to go through these stages over and over again. Sometimes you can go through all five stages in five minutes; at other times one stage will be with you for days. The only way through grief is through it. If you try to deny it or numb it with alcohol, food, or drugs, it will just hang on longer. I always suggest that you give yourself permission to experience whatever it is that you are experiencing. If you feel angry, express your anger with the writing exercise. If you are depressed, give yourself permission to crawl into the fetal position in bed and pull the covers over your head. You will come out at some point to go to the bathroom or to eat. The depression stage is a good time to do the writing exercise to express your hurt. Remember, hurt is an emotion we use to get what we want. It is important to express it and to get it out of you. If you find you are obsessing on what went wrong, then give yourself permission to really go for it. At some point, you will realize that the relationship was a powerful classroom, and you will begin to uncover what you were to learn.

Some people will understand what you are going through and can be a wonderful support, while others will be indifferent and will have no idea what to say or do. Some people will say, "Get over it. How long are you going to stay stuck in that?" Just remember that people are doing the best that they can and are offering you the best advice or direction that has been offered to them. If they truly knew better, they would do better. Don't take it personally. If someone hasn't walked through the grieving process in a healthy manner, there is no way they can assist you. Be gentle with yourself and know you are learning how to complete in a healthy way.

THE FINAL EXAM

At the end of every class, there is usually a final exam. If you pass the final exam, then you don't have to take the class over again. If you don't take the exam, then you just might have to take the class over again. Some classes we don't mind repeating, while there are some classes we hope never to experience again. Either way, it is good to complete the final exam as a way of declaring what we have learned.

There are basically three parts to the final exam in relationships. They are what I appreciated, what I learned, and what I will miss.

It's important to acknowledge and state what we appreciated because it lets us know there was value in the relationship. There were things that were precious about our partner. There were reasons we fell in love with them. It wasn't all bad or wrong. There were a lot of good things. When we complete the sentence, "What I appreciate about you is," we discover what is important to us. The things we appreciate are qualities, values, or characteristics we want in a loving relationship.

The second part—what I learned—has four subcategories: what I learned about you, what I learned about myself, what I learned about relationships, and what I learned about life. By completing these four statements, we can see where we were in denial or where we were innocent. We begin to discover who we are, what works for us, and what doesn't work for us. We move out of the "right/wrong" process of blaming and into that expanded view we talked about in the chapter on acceptance in Chapter 4. By completing these statements, we further discover what is important to us and what we want or don't want in a loving relationship. We are able to claim our learning in a very conscious, dynamic manner.

The last part—what I am going to miss—lets us acknowledge that there is a tearing here. There is an "ouch" here. We are looking at what we planned to do in the future, and we are saying that these things will not be happening. We will not be getting old together, sharing walks in the rain, watching that movie together, going to Paris, having babies, or whatever else we said we would be doing together. And yes, tears show up. We feel the grief in our hearts as we state what we are going to miss. We are not in denial; we are in truth. We are also learning who we are and what is important to us on yet another level. The things we are going to miss are often tender, sensitive, intimate moments. They are also things that are important for us in a loving relationship. We are acknowledging where we saw value and that we will miss these experiences.

Saying goodbye in a healthy, loving way is very powerful and not necessarily easy. It is, however, an important process to walk through in order to be complete. We can say goodbye in a loving way. It isn't necessary to hurt ourselves or our partner. If you trace the history of the word goodbye, you will find that it comes from an old English phrase, "God be ye" or "God be with you."

In the ideal picture, it is wonderful for two people who are parting to complete the final exam and share it with each other. When this happens, a profound sense of healing takes place on all sides. This, of course, doesn't always happen because it isn't always appropriate or safe. In these types of situations, we can still take the final exam by ourselves, and we can mock up what we think our partner would say to complete each statement. We can write down what we think they would appreciate about us, what we think they learned by being with us, and what we think they will miss now that the relationship is over. After we have written down their answers, we read them to ourselves so we can let go and move on with our life.

It is important to remember the Law of Reversibility in Chapter 5 at this point. It shows up big time at the end of a relationship. The question "Are you sure?" will show up over and over again, and it will be particularly loud on the law of reversibility time schedule of three days, one week, three weeks, three months, six months, one year, three years, and six years. Some people feel that if they are still thinking about their partner, then that means they are "supposed" to be together. This is not necessarily so. You could just be revisiting the process of the relationship in your mind as a way of completing or relearning your lessons on yet another level.

If you find yourself continuing to revisit the relationship and you don't seem to be able to move on, you can do the Blue Room Meditation.

THE BLUE ROOM MEDITATION

The Blue Room Meditation can be used as a way of cutting the emotional and psychic cords between you and another person. This process can help you maintain yourself while in a relationship, or it can help you complete a relationship.

In order to do the process, you will want to create a space where you can be alone for about ten minutes or so. Allow yourself to get comfortable, turn off any phones so you will not be disturbed, and close your eyes. Take a few deep breaths. Feel the cool air in your nose as you breathe in and the warm air in your nose as you exhale. With your eyes closed, it is nice to see yourself surrounded and protected with a cube of White light. As you allow yourself to relax, see yourself sitting in a beautiful blue room. As you look around, you will notice that the walls are blue, the ceiling is blue, and the floor is blue. At this point, notice that the air in the room is also a beautiful color of blue. Feel the presence of the blue in the room. Breathe in the blue color and breathe out the blue color. See it fill you and surround you. Breathe it down to the tips of your toes. See it in every cell of your body.

As you are breathing in and breathing out the blue air, notice that you are sitting in a chair in the room and that there is an empty chair about ten feet in front of you. You also notice that there is a closed door on the far end of the room. As you are sitting in your chair, the person you want to disconnect with opens the door, walks in, and sits in the empty chair in front of you. As they are sitting there, keep breathing the blue light in and out. Say to the person, "For the highest good of all concerned, I release with love any sexual, creative, energetic, competitive, or codependent promises that I have made with you. I reclaim myself, and I reclaim my power as a co-creator. Anything I have taken from you, I give back to you with love. I release you, and I let you go."

Visualize yourself holding a pair of scissors in your right hand and very gently and lovingly cutting any cords between you and the other person. Do this in front of you, behind you, above you, below you, and on both sides. You can assume there is a connective cord any place you have touched, they have touched, you have looked, or they have looked. Very gently cut all of these cords. As you lovingly cut these cords, place a small ball of White light on your end and on their end of the cord that you've cut as a way of sealing off the cord. As you are cutting the cords, you might notice that some of the cords are microscopic and some are huge. Just keep cutting until all of the cords are cut. For some of the cords, you might need a chain saw to cut through them. Use whatever you need to use to cut the cords. Sometimes these cords seem to reconnect after you have cut them. Just keep cutting the cords until they are all cut and remain cut, and seal each cut cord with a ball of White light.

When this process is complete, take a deep breath and again be aware of breathing the blue air in and out. Now visualize yourself holding a large magnet in your right hand. The other person is also holding a large magnet. Say, "I release all hooks, seen and unseen." Visualize seeing yourself moving the magnet in front of you, behind you, above and below, and on both sides. The other person is doing the same thing. See the hooks gently and lovingly being released and attaching to the magnet. Some of the hooks are microscopic, and some are huge. Again, you can assume there will be a hook where you or they have touched or where you or they have looked. Slowly and gently move the magnet around your body until all of the hooks have been released. Remember that this is a loving process. When all of the hooks are released, visualize planting the magnet with the attached hooks deep in the earth. The other person has been releasing any hooks you placed in them and is also planting the magnet deep in the earth.

At this point, visualize above your head a beautiful ball of White light radiating down upon you, filling all the places where the hooks have been. Notice there is a beautiful ball of White light radiating down on the other person as well, filling in any void that has been created by the removal of the hooks.

Now it is time to put a shield of protection around you and the other person. You can do this very quickly by first seeing nine layers of White light, then nine layers of purple light, then another nine layers of White light around you and the other person. Once this is complete, see the other person standing up and walking back toward the door they came in. When they get to the door, they pause, turn, and wave goodbye with a gentle smile on their face and love in their eyes. You say to them, "Let go. It's over. Go in peace." They say to you, "Let go. It's over. Go in peace." At this point, they turn and walk out the door, closing it behind them.

At this point, again be aware that you are sitting in the blue room, breathing blue air in and out. Allow the peace to settle in your heart. When you feel complete, gently bring yourself back into your current physical space. You can drink some water and wash your face to help you become present.

You might need to do this exercise up to thirty-two times to fully complete the process of letting go. Each time, it will be easier and faster. The key here is to be gentle with yourself as you learn to let go in a gentle, loving way.

THIRTY-TWO-DAY CALENDAR

Monday	Tuesday	Wednesday	Thursday	Friday	Saturday	Sunday
♥	♥	♥	♥	♥	♥	♥
♥	♥	♥	♥	♥	♥	♥
♥	♥	♥	♥	♥	♥	♥
♥	♥	♥	♥	♥	♥	♥
♥	♥	♥	♥	♥	♥	♥

HEALING OF MEMORIES INVOLVING INTIMATE RELATIONSHIPS

This is a good place to pause and do a healing of memory exercise on past relationships. As I suggested earlier, many of us have been told that only relationships that last a lifetime are successful and that anything less than that is a failure, suggesting that if we have had relationships that have lasted only a few months or a few years, then we are failures at having relationships. We begin to think, "There must be something wrong with me." We begin to think we have a history of failed relationships. By doing the healing of memory exercise and going back through time, we can complete each relationship in a healthy, loving way. Each relationship can be a learning experience and a growth opportunity for all concerned. As a result, we can create a history of successful relationships. We can use each relationship as a steeping stone to heal our inner issues and to learn how to communicate our wants with someone we love deeply. We can learn that being vulnerable and open has value. We can learn that we can be our true selves.

As you do any healing of memory exercise, use your thirty-two-day calendar to track your progress. In order to gain the most value, it is important to do the exercise every day consecutively for thirty-two days. As you heal your past relationships and complete them in a healthy, loving way, you might want to start at the beginning with your first love and then move forward in time until you are current and complete with every intimate relationship you have experienced. Or you can jump around doing the ones that have the most charge for you. Do what works best for you.

AN EXAMPLE

As I go back in time, I remember my first girlfriend when I was in first grade. I remember giving her a Christmas present, and she gave me a present as well. I see us talking and sharing about life as first graders do, and we share our appreciation for each other. We talk about learning to give and receive and to be polite and to listen. We say goodbye, wishing each other the best. There isn't much to miss at this point. We are just enjoying the gentle sweetness of early childhood. The relationship was very successful. No one was hurt or abandoned. We parted and moved on in our lives.

The next day, I see myself sharing a Valentine's Day card with the girl in my third-grade class. She smiled when I gave her a card, and she also gave a card to me. We talked briefly and giggled. That was about the extent of that relationship. I reflect on how wonderful it was to be appreciated by her and how exciting it was to give a card to her. Love was exchanged in a moment, and life moved on.

For the next several days, I review many of those early moments of puppy love, and each encounter is completed with words of appreciation, learning, and missing.

I now move into the teenage years, and I remember the dance. There she was. My heart stood still. I walked across the dance floor, and she said she would dance with me. We danced and laughed and talked. We spoke on the phone. We dated. We held hands. We kissed. Time passed, and we realized we were both complete. We shared all the learning, all the love, all the moments of tenderness. We healed the times where miscommunication had occurred. We explored the concept of jealousy and fear. We learned to say goodbye in a loving way. We held each other as we let go of each other so we could experience more of life.

For the next week, I slowly work my way through these early years of teenage love. So many decisions about life and relationships are reviewed and revised. My teenager has learned so much at this point. I feel ready to move into adulthood.

I explore the courtship and relationship of a marriage. All the learning of living with another person is reexperienced. I review and heal the hurt, the misunderstanding, the abandonment, the betrayal, and finally the divorce. Much time is spent here. Some old hurt and anger surfaces, and I do a lot of writing and burning to release the suppressed emotions that are surfacing. I work through the process of acceptance, and I come to a place of peace and understanding. I see us talking and sharing what we appreciate about each other, what we have learned, and what we will miss. I feel complete, and I move on with a sense of knowing that everything happened so I could grow and become more of who I truly am.

I feel complete. My thirty-two-day process is almost over. I look back through time and revisit a few of the earlier relationships with more wisdom. As I finish, I feel complete. I have healed my past relationship issues. I feel ready to move on with my life, and I am at peace with my past. I know how to have a relationship, I know I have more to learn, and I am capable and willing to open my heart to another.

CHAPTER 12

Three Metaphors to Remember

*T*ogether we've explored a lot of things in this book. We discussed what feelings are, how they are used and ways to express them in a healthy manner, so we don't hurt ourselves or others. We learned to listen to our self-talk, how our self-talk affects us, as well as others, and how to effectively change our negative self-talk to positive self-talk. Next we discovered several ways how we keep ourselves stuck in behaviors that no longer serve us. After that we revealed keys to getting ourselves unstuck so we can begin to get more of what we want in our lives. From there we discussed the various patterns to be aware of that can seem larger than life; patterns that just don't seem to go away. We uncovered the concept of boundaries, what they are and how to set them effectively so we can honor ourselves and others in relationships. This took us to methods to stay clear and focused as we move through our lives. We then journeyed into the past and explored how to change past experiences and how to heal those memories that have kept us stuck. And finally, we ventured into the world of relationships, what a healthy relationship looks like and how to maintain this healthy relationship through time.

All of this might seem overwhelming. It might seem like too much information and/or too much work to do. If this is what you are experiencing then let me share three short metaphors that capture a lot of what I have written, so when all is said and done, you just have to remember three concepts.

Number One: If I want orange juice, I have to go where orange juice is. If I go to the kitchen sink and turn on the faucet, I'll get water. I don't care how much I kick and spit, I will still just get water. If I want orange juice, I have to get some oranges and squeeze out the juice, get a can of orange concentrate and add water, or go to the store and buy a container of orange juice. Orange juice does not come out of my faucet.

What does this mean? It means people are who they are. They are not who we want them to be; they are simply who they are. It is not our job to make them into what we want them to be. They are not their potential. They are who they are. We are changing all of the time, but we're still who we are. If I want you to be something other than who you are, I will be disappointed. If I can celebrate who you are, accept you for who you are, and love you for being who you are, then we will be just fine. If not, then we will have problems. If I want something different, then I will need to go find someone else who can give me something different.

Number Two: There's a nursery rhyme that we all know and sang when we were children. It is very profound. It goes like this:

Row, row, row your boat

Gently down the stream

Merrily, merrily, merrily

Life is but a dream

We are to row our boat down the stream, not up the stream or across the stream. When we row our boat down the stream, life is present. Life is easy. And life is but a dream filled with joy. However, if we row our boat up the stream, we are not present in our lives. Life is not easy. And life is anything but a dream. Maybe we're not supposed to take life so seriously.

Sometimes we feel we must have it our way. We feel this is the only person or place in the whole world where we can get what we want. We know we are an exception to the rule. We know if we just do it "right," we will be successful. Everyone tells us this is not true, but we know we can get what we want and insist on doing it our way. We feel rowing upstream is the right thing; in fact, we feel it is the only thing we can do. We have to do it. No matter what! Period! We insist on getting orange juice from a faucet.

This brings me to the third and last metaphor to remember.

Number Three: Let's say I have several dogs. I love my dogs. They are the best. I let them play in my backyard all the time, and if you're a dog owner, then you know that dogs do what dogs do. From time to time, they relieve themselves. I must tell you it's OK with me, because I love my dogs. However, there's something about me that I must share with you. I hate cleaning up dog poop. I hate it. So I don't. Never do. I won't get close to the stuff. Now there's something else that I must share about me. This is pretty secret stuff, but I can tell you. My secret is that I love to walk barefoot in my backyard when it's pitch dark. I'm not sure why. It just does something for me. It's the only thing that does it. The only problem is that I get dog poop in between my toes when I walk in my backyard barefoot at night. I can't figure it out. Yuck! I hate it. What to do?

Now I have a couple of choices. I could get rid of my dogs. Nope. That is not an option. I couldn't live without my dogs. So that's out. I could pick up the dog poop. No way. I already told you I don't even want to get close to that stuff. So that's out. What to do? I bitch and complain a lot. I have yelled and screamed. I have kicked and spit. None of that seemed to work. I could stop walking in my backyard at night barefoot. No. That's out. I told you it is the only thing that really does it for me. So I have to keep doing that. I could hire someone to pick up my backyard. No, that won't work because I don't like other people in my backyard. Hmm. What to do?

I have two other options. One, I could enjoy the dog poop between my toes. It could be an experience I could learn to accept. I could use the acceptance model and change my attitude to gratitude by changing my altitude. Dog poop in toes means I have great dogs. No dog poop in toes means I don't have dogs. Or two, I could realize that when I walk in my backyard barefoot at night, I will get dog poop between my toes. It goes with the territory. I just have to wash my feet before I put on my shoes. If I pretend that I will not step in the stuff, that I am an exception to the rule, then I will be disappointed and angry. Life will be challenging.

So here are the final keys to joy filled living: know where to get orange juice, row your boat down the stream, and if you insist on walking barefoot in your backyard; wash your feet before you put on your shoes.

Life can be a dream filled with joy.

About The Author

ROBERT C. JAMESON, MFT

As a licensed marriage and family therapist, Robert C. Jameson focuses on helping clients understand and overcome issues, such as anger, hurt, depression, anxiety, love, relationships, boundaries and limiting beliefs, to name a few. During his years of private practice, Mr. Jameson found it useful to give many of his clients "homework" in the form of handouts to support their work while in session. *The Keys to Joy-Filled Living* was born from his handout of tried and true exercises and techniques.

Mr. Jameson is also the author of *Thoughts of Pomery*, an entertaining book of pictures and thoughts that guides the reader to expand their perceptions of life and relationships with others, *Don't Lose Weight — Give It Away*, which explores the emotional aspects of weight loss, and *The Pocket Oasis*, a fun and useful pocket-sized book that can be used as a tool to help center anyone during a hectic day.

In addition to his work as a therapist and writer, Mr. Jameson is an accomplished musician. He recently produced and released, *Ani Hu — Empathy with God*, an hour-long CD, which helps the listener to meditate, relax, or sleep.

For more information please visit: www.thekeystojoyfilledliving.com.

Free Bonus Material

for The *Keys* To *Joy*-Filled *Living*

Working with and understanding The Keys to Joy-Filled Living is both a rewarding and ongoing experience. To help you "stay the course," we've created exciting bonus materials to help with your continued success in all areas of your life. Visit us at www.TheKeysToJoyFilledLiving.com/AdvancedKeys.

- Learn how to create that relationship, job or that ideal home
- Uncover the limiting beliefs that block you from getting what you want
- Discover how to create expansive beliefs that will set you free
- Create a method that reprograms your unconscious
- And much more

In addition to creating a wonderful joy-filled life, help us to create a joy-filled world! How? Easy!

Tell a friend about The Keys!

That's right! Each time you tell friends and loved ones about The Keys to Joy- Filled Living, you help to create a joy-filled world…one friend at a time. It's that simple.

And don't forget to join our "Weekly Blog Theme Team," designed to keep you motivated as you create your way to a successful joy-filled life!

http://www.TheKeysToJoyFilledLiving.com/AdvancedKeys

BUY A SHARE OF THE FUTURE IN YOUR COMMUNITY

These certificates make great holiday, graduation and birthday gifts that can be personalized with the recipient's name. The cost of one S.H.A.R.E. or one square foot is $54.17. The personalized certificate is suitable for framing and will state the number of shares purchased and the amount of each share, as well as the recipient's name. The home that you participate in "building" will last for many years and will continue to grow in value.

Here is a sample SHARE certificate:

THIS CERTIFIES THAT

YOUR NAME HERE

HAS INVESTED IN A HOME FOR A DESERVING FAMILY

1985-2005

TWENTY YEARS OF BUILDING FUTURES IN OUR
COMMUNITY ONE HOME AT A TIME

1200 SQUARE FOOT HOUSE @ $65,000 = $54.17 PER SQUARE FOOT
This certificate represents a tax deductible donation. It has no cash value.

YES, I WOULD LIKE TO HELP!

I support the work that Habitat for Humanity does and I want to be part of the excitement! As a donor, I will receive periodic updates on your construction activities but, more importantly, I know my gift will help a family in our community realize the dream of homeownership. I would like to SHARE in your efforts against substandard housing in my community! (Please print below)

PLEASE SEND ME _____ SHARES at $54.17 EACH = $ $_____

In Honor Of: _____

Occasion: (Circle One)   HOLIDAY   BIRTHDAY   ANNIVERSARY

OTHER: _____

Address of Recipient: _____

Gift From: _____ *Donor Address:* _____

Donor Email: _____

I AM ENCLOSING A CHECK FOR $ $_____ PAYABLE TO HABITAT FOR HUMANITY OR PLEASE CHARGE MY VISA OR MASTERCARD *(CIRCLE ONE)*

Card Number _____ Expiration Date: _____

Name as it appears on Credit Card _____ Charge Amount $ _____

Signature _____

Billing Address _____

Telephone # Day _____ Eve _____

PLEASE NOTE: Your contribution is tax-deductible to the fullest extent allowed by law.
Habitat for Humanity • P.O. Box 1443 • Newport News, VA 23601 • 757-596-5553
www.HelpHabitatforHumanity.org

Printed in the United States
144825LV00005B/19/P